The Off-Season
for Financial Advisors

The Off-Season for Financial Advisors

The Industry Secrets Your Executive Coach Better Be Telling You

By
Walter Bond and Rich Campe
with Todd Mauney

The Off-Season for Financial Advisors™ is a trademark of Motivation Made Easy Publishing, Motivation Made Easy Publications, Walter Bond Seminars, Rich Campe Intl., LLC, and ProAdvisor Coach denoting a series of products that may include but is not limited to books, audio products, video products, pocket cards, calendars, t-shirts, coffee mugs and more.

Published by:

Motivation Made Easy Publishing
A subsidiary of Walter Bond Seminars, Inc.
Minneapolis, MN

www.walterbond.com

Printed in the United States of America.

ISBN: 0-9787805-1-5

The Inspiration for the Off-Season Playbook

Walter Bond

I have been encouraged by some of America's top thought leaders to create and write a line of self-help books called "The Off-Season" and make it a reality. I have partnered with Rich Campe, CEO of ProAdvisor Coach, whose company has the best coaching program for Advisors in the industry that I have seen to date. In this book, we will translate the concepts of an Off-Season and tailor it just for Financial Advisors, Producers, Managers and Insurance Agents. For the sake of continuity in this book, we will refer to you as an Advisor.

It was May 2008 and I was attending a conference in Minneapolis with the National Speakers Association. This was not our annual July conference, or just another meeting open to membership. This conference was a high-end think tank for the top members of the association. It was by invitation only. This meeting was designated for about sixty of the top influential leaders. I found out later that I only got invited to the conference because another speaker cancelled and I received a last minute invite. This was fitting, as it has become the story of my life. I have always been an afterthought and I don't mind crashing a party. The NBA did not initially invite me and I crashed that party too!

I'm not usually easily intimidated, to put it bluntly, I was a little nervous as I entered the room with Americas top thought leaders. Why? I don't want to name drop, but these were the leaders that have their books located prominently in every bookstore in America. How did I get in this room? In the six billion dollar training and development world this was All-Star weekend. Do I belong here? I teach confidence at every presentation I deliver and I was in awe to say the least. I needed someone to remind me of my own message of "confidence is arrogance under control" right here-right now.

We were actually given a homework assignment prior to the conference - to come up with a million dollar idea. How about that? I had to come up with a million dollar idea then present it to the leaders whom have already had multi-million dollar ideas. These leaders have had ideas that they've already translated into multi-million dollar businesses. Was I starting to feel intimidated? You can bet I was! As the presentations progressed, I started to regain my confidence about my own idea. I ended up being the last person in my group to present and recall vividly the moment in which I stood up slowly with a lump in my throat and sweat on my brow to give my presentation called "The Off-Season." I gave a presentation about an idea of changing the culture of America, one person at a time, one company at a time and one family at a time. I actually stood up in front of America's most influential thought leaders and presented a revolutionary concept challenging the way we live in America today. What a bold attempt by a person that nobody even knew. Would I be perceived as militant, radical, brilliant or just plain dumb? As we transitioned out of the room into the hallway for a break, I was relieved that it was over. I was glad I didn't embarrass myself in front of such brilliant minds. Throughout the day many of these top leaders grabbed me in the hallway during the breaks and told me that they loved my presentation. They thought that I was on to something big. They said, "You better write this book before somebody else beats you to it." My confidence has soared about the scope of this project ever since. Almost everyone at the conference grabbed me at some point during the weekend and validated my million-dollar idea. They told me that I am the only one with the background and credibility to pull it off. I immediately reclaimed my "Walter Bond All-State from Chicago" strut. This book is an extension of that amazing weekend spent with brilliant people. This is our expression to America's professionals in the Financial Industry. This book is our heart and soul, our contribution to your financial world. We need every Advisor to read this book and execute its basic principles.

If you think about it for a moment, we are all after the same things – more success, financial stability and fulfillment. Collectively we need to rebuild America's trust in investing and investment products. I have been the opening speaker at MDRT, I have presented at GAMA, and I have about 100 speaking events each year. I have or will present to almost every major financial firm or institution in America, so I've learned how Advisors think. This "The Off-Season Playbook" has been written specifically for Insurance and Financial Advisors, Producers, Managers and Agents like you. This idea has been stirring within me for a long time and has come to fruition with the help of Rich Campe and his associates.

This book has the power to transform your world professionally. We wrote this book with the hope of starting the revolution in the financial industry. First we want to gain our country back financially, and then gain our family and our children back, while not forgetting our mind, body and soul. America needs to be inspired to reclaim its rightful position as the world's leader in industry, innovation and lifestyle. As an Advisor you will naturally want to build a nice book of business but in a larger scope you have been armed with the charge of rebuilding America's financial future.

The economy has scared people away from investing and building a sound financial portfolio. If you aren't careful it can cripple your ability to build your book of business. We are dealing with the Madoff affect. America has lost confidence in financial professionals. We think that every Advisor who rings the doorbell may be the next Bernie Madoff, the former Investment Advisor who defrauded $65 billion from his clients. When we watch the news, talk about life with our friends or just pay attention to the world around us, we get more and more convinced that we aren't just spiraling out of control as a nation…we are there. We are out of control already. Our economy has waned, I don't necessarily buy into recessions because our money hasn't disappeared. Many of you just can't find it. However, the reality is that people think we are in a recession so in many people's minds there is one. We will not be teaching the sales techniques I cover in my seminars, but here is one cliff note: Please! Stop selling tangible products. Start selling hopes and dreams! We all have corporate pressure at work to produce at a high level so we can keep our jobs and keep climbing our own personal success ladder. Why? So we can live in the house we want to live in, drive the car that we want to drive, take exotic trips or just give it all away as a philanthropist. I am sure you would like to win the awards at your company's functions. You may be saying to yourself that you want to qualify for the MDRT next year or move into a management roll with your current company. We all want to show well and look good. When you are doing well the class reunion is great and attending it is a non-issue. When we aren't doing well and looking good do you want to go? We all want a quality of life that is congruent with our self-worth, self- esteem and vision we had way back in the sixth grade. We long for the dream life we see on TV. However, after a long day of work and coming up short, do we get to relax when work is over? Of course not! We want to raise perfect kids, so we run off to every gymnasium, soccer field, piano lesson or auditorium to support our children. We want to prepare them to compete in this very competitive world, even though they have no clue what awaits their future. The pressure causes you to yell at the referees, yell at the coach and even yell at your child if they didn't excel up to our pre-conceived suburban expectations. Then, we rush home to stuff down an unhealthy and quick dinner while we stand at the counter. There is no time to sit down as a family anymore and break bread. No time to debrief the day and hear about what happened on the school bus or lunch room. After dinner it's homework time, so we help with homework. In some extreme cases we actually do it for them depending on your child's level of brilliance or your need to celebrate their success. I have sat in classrooms during my children's presentations and it is painfully obvious that a few of the kids did not do the assignment themselves. I have seen projects laced with adult language and context that is way above the intellect of a sixth grader. There is nothing cute about an over barring and over powering parent not allowing the child to fail or take charge themselves. Most suburban kids don't even possess the skills to organize and play a game outside in their neighborhood. They are so used to the helicopter parent that is always hovering around trying to raise that perfect child. After the nightly homework is done, do we get to rest? Wrong again. We have to connect with our spouse and keep our hopes of a successful marriage or relationship alive. We hope and pray we never resemble an episode of the Jerry Springer TV Show in front of our children. Most of us collapse during the news. As you drift off to sleep, feeling somewhat good about your productive day, you hear that P90X infomercial guy talk about physical fitness. You realize that in your jam packed day you didn't even work out. You're busy from sun up to sun down and you still didn't get it all in. You have been longing for the day your physical body returns to its glory days. Remember when you could actually go to the beach or the pool without covering up? You have to figure out a way to fit a workout into your insanely busy day. How? You almost have it all and are barely holding it all together. You feel close to meltdown or breakdown, whichever comes first.

Now, it's the weekend and you think that maybe you can rest, but you are locked in all day with activities. You follow your children to game after game, and their competitions suck up the entire weekend. You attend travel soccer games, basketball games, gymnastics or long track meets in the blazing hot sun. You and your spouse have to split up to cover all the kids' activities. Now it's finally Sunday, the Lord's Day of rest. So, we use Sunday not as a day of rest but literally as a day of collapse, unless there are more kids activities. If possible, you sleep in. You are worn out from the pace of the week and you still don't have it all. There is something still missing, it is still not coming all together. What's missing? You're constantly asking yourself, I had a great week so why do I feel a void? Even though you got some much needed rest, Sunday is not really peaceful because you didn't go to church, mass or to the synagogue and even worse, your children didn't go either. You know deep down inside that you need to go to your place of worship to fill your spiritual tank. Both of you lay in the bed content to just lay there hoping the other doesn't bring it up. The guiltiest one brings it up, "Hey honey, are we going to church?" You want to say no, and briefly hate your spouse for even bringing it up. You say, "let's just lay here and recap the week and connect" or "how about we enjoy a bedside church service on TV like Joel Osteen?". You never planned on being a bible banger but you know you should have God as a part of your life. Attending your house of worship helps to strengthen that relationship. You take in a bedside service on TV to make the guilt go away, but it isn't quite the same as being there. You worry that your children will be spiritual misfits and it's your fault. They have no clue what faith is really all about because you almost never attend services. Sundays are the only day you can slow it all down. You've become CEO's, and not of your own company. You are a CEO of your Faith. You only attend your place of worship on Christmas, Easter and Other important holidays. Sunday can be a day of grief when it should be a day to rejoice. You are worn out by the week of sales calls trying to grow your book of business and everything else that goes with life. So you skipped church but at least you got some rest.

You are on the go all day long, working hard for your clients and family but are still coming up short. How do you get it all? How do you pull this thing all together? You want it all but it is so elusive. America, listen up! Keeping up this pace has worn us all out! We are on the go all of the time but still can't quite get it all together. Over time, this leads to depression, despair, frustration, divorce, obesity and the feeling of being unfulfilled. Our pace is deafening and yet we keep this pace up year after year. When one of these areas isn't quite right it eats at the core of you. You don't feel like a disappointment but you feel disappointed because you are so close to what you want but yet so far. You are tired, stale, dull and no matter how busy you seem to be. When does the madness end? You attend a conference like MDRT or GAMA. It is good see everyone but when you return home it all hits you again. When was the last time you and your spouse went out on a date? When was the last time you took a trip that was not a company sponsored incentive trip? Are you, your spouse and your family growing apart? Meanwhile, no significant progress is being made in your business. It will get better once the children are out of the house. We all want the same things, right? Why is euphoria so elusive? Is it possible to have it all? Can we have it all? Yes! I am greedy, I want it all and I believe we can have it all. The impact of this book will lift a nation and empower every Advisor to live the life they dream about at work and at home. This book will give you hope that you can have it all. Wherever you are in life….it's not your lot in life. It is a pit stop on your journey to euphoria. I don't want you to taper your expectation one bit. God told us to be fruitful and multiply. By Golly, if He says it, I believe it can be done. The concepts in this book will help you find the solutions to grow your business by merely creating an Off-Season just like Michael Jordan, Magic Johnson and Cal Ripken. This book won't go inept into challenges such as family issues and overall success in all life's disciplines, those answers can be found in our foundational book "The Off-Season." The focus of "The Off-Season for Financial Advisors" is on core business concepts that you all need to focus on. This lifestyle book was inspired by what I learned during my athletic career that began on the south side of Chicago.

After a stellar high school basketball career at Whitney Young and Collins High School in Chicago I accepted a scholarship to attend the University of Minnesota and play for the Golden Gophers. I was an All-State basketball player growing up in Chicago. Whenever I played basketball the gymnasium was jam packed. I can still hear my classmates standing on their feet and chanting my name when I walked into the gym. "Walter.... Walter.... Walter!" Ok, I may be exaggerating a little. We had a really good team and I was considered one of the top players in the country. I was recruited by schools all over the America; Michigan, Minnesota, Wisconsin, UCLA, and Arizona State. I had many choices of colleges but I finally settled on the University of Minnesota. When I walked on campus I thought I was God's gift to basketball and to the University of Minnesota for that matter. That is, until I met my first teammate. I will never forget that experience because I was still full of confidence the day I met him and introduced myself. I said very confidently, "My name is Walter Bond All-State from Chicago". In other words, the Messiah has arrived! My teammate stood up and looked down at me with a menacing glare and said "Walter Bond All-State from Chicago"? "My name is Willie Burton All-American from Detroit!!!!" Did he say All-American? Surely there is an easy explanation, because in my juvenile mind I was supposed to be the star here just like in high school. I also noticed that he was three inches taller and we played the same position.

I didn't think much of it because of all the confidence I had stored up from years past. At that point in my life, everything I had touched had turned into gold. I had never experienced failure in sports or anything else for that matter up until this point of my life so I expected success to continue. I was always the best basketball player on just about every basketball court I had ever played. I was Walter Bond All-State from Chicago. At our first practice my goal was to find the toughest guy on the team, take the basketball and dunk it right in his face to establish that I was be the star here too. When I entered the locker room I found the toughest guy on the team, his name was Richard Coffey. Richard Coffey was 6'6, 235 pounds and was a former member of the 82nd Airborne. If you aren't familiar with the 82nd Airborne, it is an exclusive Paratrooping unit out of Fort Bragg, NC. When I saw his body up close it was the first time I questioned God. I thought we were all created equal. Richard Coffey was a grown man sitting in that locker room. I honestly couldn't tell him from the coaches, they all looked the same to me. I figured it was finally time for me to become a man and establish myself at this new level. My plan was to take the basketball and dunk it in Richard Coffey's face at my first opportunity. Bring it on Richard Coffey, bring it on Uncle Sam. I grabbed the ball and went in with everything I had. Right before I got to the rim Richard Coffey met me in mid- air...Bam! Splat! Boom!

Down I went....I was slammed down to the ground. Richard stood over me and said "82nd Airborne we do it all...first to fight, last to fall, get up you little freshman." Before that practice ended, Richard confirmed he could knock me down whenever he felt like it.

So there you have it, that is how my college career began, needless to say I did not play very much as a freshman. I found myself in a place I never thought I would be. Have you been there yourself? Is your career where you thought it would be? Is your marriage where you thought it would be? Is your family life where you thought it would be? Did you ever think your body would be where it is today? Never thought you would develop a gut like your dad did? You are becoming your mom and you can't believe it. You never thought you would actually start looking like those moms at school picking up their kids. When I grew up, every mom ranged from being a little plump to very obese. My fantasy was to always be the good looking dad that all the girls had a secret crush on because I still looked young, cool and hip.

My freshman year I was very frustrated and disappointed. I had a sadness that rested deep in my soul as I sat there game after game on the bench at the University of Minnesota. My once strong mind was bombarded by a litany of negative thoughts going through my head as the games piled up and I rotted on the bench. Is this my lot in life? I thought it would be different than this; maybe I'm not as good as I thought. Can I really play at this level? Do I have what it takes to play in the NBA? Should I just give up on my NBA dreams and just get a good education? Disappointment soon turned into justification. I was on a college scholarship. How many people could say that? Only 2% of high school athletes even get a scholarship. When we experience setbacks human nature will encourage us to justify ourselves. Hey, my marriage isn't perfect but at least I am not divorced. I am not a top producer but at least I have a job. However, no matter how hard I tried, I couldn't stomach sitting on the bench. I struggled emotionally for the first time in my life. Should I settle where I am and reconcile it in my mind or go for more? My dream was to play in the NBA, not just play college basketball. Am I technically even playing college basketball? I never get to play! Haven't you faced similar crossroads in your life? You met disappointment but instead of persevering you take the easy way out and recalibrated your dreams? You aren't where you want to be but you have vacillated between disappointment and justification. Maybe you want to take your business to the next level but you are stuck. Your career is stuck in neutral, you are not going forward or backwards. You are just towing the company line day after day hoping that something will miraculously get better but you have no real plan to swing the pendulum your way. You're so stuck between disappointment and justification. You can tell people anything they want to hear.....but you can't run from yourself. However, now you can blame everything on the economy. My business is down because of the economy. If you have your business all together and your life is absolutely perfect, this book is not the book for you. If your life is not quite where you want it, you are more than welcome to join the Off-Season revolution. We are looking for Advisors that know they are leaving meat on the bone. If you know you have more opportunities within your business, then this book is for you!

All of these thoughts and more raced through my mind as I sat on the bench and pondered my own life. I didn't like where I was but worse for me was not knowing what I was going to do about it. I was depressed, sad and embarrassed all at the same time. This derailment of my dreams was huge and I didn't even see it coming. I felt blindsided by life. My reality was something I didn't expect, it snuck up on me. I tried to hide the pain by partying and doing what college kids do, but that only made it worse. If you saw me in public I always had a smile on my face, if you asked how things were going I would always say "fine, good". When I look back on it, I was lying right through my teeth. Life wasn't bad but it wasn't good either, life was just ok. I don't like ok, and I was in somewhat of a stupor with no plan...no hope. I had an "I've fallen and I can't get up" kinda thing going on. My life was stuck, is your business stuck or life in a similar holding pattern?

At the end of the season I sat down with my coach Clem

Haskins. I was fighting back my tears as he gave me feedback about the season and about me as a basketball player. My whole self esteem and self worth was from being a successful athlete and now I have been relegated to being a scrub on the bench. "Walter, this is why you don't play for me son. You can't run, jump, dribble, shoot or rebound son." Now if you don't understand basketball, he basically listed every skill set associated with basketball. Just when I thought things were bad, my coach seemed to take me even lower. I felt like I was on the ropes and he was about to deliver the Mike Tyson knock-out punch. The meeting was short and sweet and only lasted 10 minutes as another teammate waited in the hallway to receive his performance review. I was emotionally distraught, punch drunk, almost out for the count and preparing for the final right cross to the chin when Coach Haskins said "Son, I want you to work on these things in your Off-Season and improve. If you improve in these areas, you will get more playing time next year. This is another level from High School son, this Off-Season is critical for your development. I recruited you based on your potential. You are not that far away!" All of a sudden, I had a ray of hope, he didn't deliver the knockout punch like I anticipated, and he actually gave me hope. The sun slightly cracked through the clouds. My basketball dreams received CPR and were placed on life support. If you pull the plug on a person's dreams, you pull the plug on their life. All I could hear was, "Walter if, you work on these things in your Off-Season, you will play more next season". I couldn't sleep that night; I lay awake in my bed all night with my mind racing. I knew what was at stake. This Off-Season was my chance. I am not a bench warmer, I am an impact person.

As a motivational speaker, I was my first client. I had to encourage myself, I began to speak hope to myself. I am at a new level. I'm more competitive than ever so I must do things differently to be successful at a higher level. When you are in a competitive industry you must be willing to do the things that others won't do. If you want your business to go to another level, maybe you need an Off-Season too.

When I was in High School I played all sports year round. I played them well and was very competitive. I never really needed to train for each sport or each season. I was always competing and didn't really understand what an Off-Season was all about. I was naturally better than most in every sport and enjoyed success at each. I never trained; I just played the sport in season. I went from one sport to the next like a square dance. I needed to figure this Off-Season thing out, because I was up against some stiffer competition. The financial services industry is more competitive than ever, you can beat your competition just by incorporating an Off-Season into your business practice. I strongly recommend that you have a coach as an advisor and mentor. This is why I have partnered with Rich Campe of ProAdvisor Coach to write this amazing book. Rich and his staff are the best I have come across in the industry at coaching Advisors. Their MindScan assessment alone taught me how my mind operated. Rich coached me himself and it has changed how I do business. Yes, I still take Off-Seasons. Rich helped me personally and after the coaching experience I knew that every Advisor should take the MindScan. They should enroll in their coaching program for their own Off-Season. If not Rich Campe and his associate coaches with ProAdvisor Coach, you should have someone coaching you to help grow your business. We all have blind spots and Rich helped me with mine. My college basketball coach Clem Haskins changed my world with his suggestions. That is what a good coach is supposed to do.

That meeting with Coach Haskins was my escape hatch off the path of average. My life had been very successful up to this point on natural ability, I could show up and the magic would happen. I was in a very different place and I can tell you I didn't like where I was. I hated it!!! If there is an area of your life you want to improve you better learn to hate it, if you don't hate it you won't ever change it. Have you been there yourself? Are you there right now? I was willing to do something about it. Are you? After hearing Coach Haskins suggestions, the next five months were the most important stretch of my basketball life. What I did in the Off-Season was going to influence my basketball career. I faced reality that I was an

average college basketball player and the NBA is not full of average
players. I needed to become someone different. I needed to become
a stand out. I needed to go from being a college reserve to becoming one of the top 450 basketball players in the world. If you want
to become a stand out Advisor or one of the top 450 Advisors in
the world-you need an Off-Season. I wanted to get off that bench
so bad; I couldn't let the Off-Season go to waste. I knew I must get
my basketball career off life support and back in the land of the
living. If I would ever play in the NBA these next five months were
critical. This Off-Season concept is one I needed to embrace and
make work.

We wrote this book to give you hope about your future in financial services as Advisor. Your future will be based on your successful
Off-Seasons. There is no doubt in my mind that this may be the
best book you will ever read as an Advisor. It is the answer you have
been looking for with your business direction. I know what it feels
like to not have hope or to be stuck and it stinks. I am thoroughly
convinced we can all have the life we want. We can have the salary
we want, have the wonderful kids we want, live in the house we
want, drive the car we want, have the lifestyle we want, and the only
way we can have it is by taking an Off-Season. America...we need
an Off-Season as nation. I assume that we would all agree that our
government could use an Off-Season; our entire educational system needs an Off-Season. When I think about it, an Off-Season is
the only reason I am living the life I live right now. An Off-Season
will kick start your imagination and position you to dream again.

After my freshman year in college and my first successful Off-
Season, I have never looked back. My commitment to my Off-
Seasons' have been the most important part of my personal success.
I went on to become a very productive college basketball player and
enjoyed an eight year professional basketball career in the NBA
playing for the Utah Jazz, Dallas Mavericks and Detroit Pistons.
In fact, I am still heavily involved in the NBA in player develop-
ment. I am a featured speaker for the NBA rookies every year in
New York City and various other NBA programs. My Off-Seasons

have created a platform that has placed me in front of great people and afforded me a great lifestyle in posh hotels and private planes. I didn't stop my Off-Seasons after my basketball playing days ended. I have incorporated them into my business and have enjoyed the benefits ever since. My Off-Seasons have created a dream life that you can have too.

Every year at the University of Minnesota, I was voted most improved player. I took my Off-Seasons very seriously as a college athlete. As an athlete I couldn't wait for the season to end so my Off-Season could begin. If my Off-Season was successful my season was equally as successful. You should become your company's most improved Advisor every year. I am in control of life's track now; you can be in control of yours too. If there is something in my life that isn't up to my standards, it no longer frustrates me. I have a mechanism in place to do something about it. We can win America back one person at a time. We must all change how we live and adopt a lifestyle that includes an Off-Season. Here is the answer…read this book, incorporate its principles and pass it on to every Advisor at your company. You will see your company get off the treadmill, exit the rat race and take back control. The hope of this book is to see all financial services companies see continuous improvement and reclaim our nation financially one family at a time. You can have the life you have dreamed about when your company appointed you to become an Advisor. The key is for you to take an Off-Season. Rich Campe, his team, and myself will show you what you should do in your Off-Season as an Advisor to achieve maximum success each and every year. Enjoy!

Congratulations!

————————

First, we would like to commend you for choosing to begin your new journey to embark on a higher level of awareness and success. Simply by choosing to invest in the "Off-Season Playbook," you have joined a select group of individuals that **do** versus the majority of people who *don't*.

Like those who have gone before you, we are certain that you will find the entire process extremely rewarding. Please be aware that some individuals might experience minor frustration and confusion during the early stages of the process. However, it's important that you don't get discouraged. Remember, this is a journey of discovery and should be treated as if you are a detective, investigative reporter or archeologist in search of lost treasure. The clues and lost treasure are within you and your business and it's our job as coaches to help draw out the best clues and treasure from within yourself. It's your job to keep the course and enjoy the journey.

As you gain new awareness of your inner self and try new skills, it's normal to experience *frustration* and some discomfort.

It's important to remember that...

"Nothing in life has any meaning except the **meaning you give it**."

A valid definition of frustration is...

"I am about to learn something new."

We will never forget watching our children learn to walk. They would trip, stumble and fall hundreds of times before eventually acquiring the skills to walk. The important part is they eventually learned how to walk, skip, and even run. You could say that like most children they actually mastered the "art of walking." We are all on a journey of discovery, adventure and mastery. Someone helped coach all of us to walk and they did not give up on us until we succeeded... so let's not give up on each other and ourselves.

The four levels of learning that you will experience with any new adventure are:

Unconscious Incompetence – This is when you don't even realize you are doing something wrong. When our kids first learned to ride bikes they did not even know what the pedals were for or how to hold the handlebars. In fact, we can even remember having to explain what a bicycle does.

Conscious Incompetence – This is the stage when you realize what you did not know or understand; when you realize what you might have been doing wrong. Again, using our kids as an example, there was a moment in time when they first discovered both the correct and incorrect way to sit on the bike. By pedaling backwards the brakes became engaged, and if they don't hold onto the handlebars they crash. In essence they were consciously aware of **what not to do**.

Conscious Competence – This is the stage when you think about what you are actually doing and performing that activity correctly, or in the desired manner. You're consciously competent and aware of your thinking, decisions, and actions. Our kids learned that pedaling the bike in a forward motion resulted in their travelling forward. When they hold onto the handlebars and look in the direction they want to head and continue to pedal, they achieve their desired outcome of riding the bike.

<u>Unconscious Competence</u> – This is the stage when you do not even think about what to do - you "Just Do It". Your unconscious mind knows what needs to be done and you do it. This is the part of the brain that enables your heart to beat over 115,000 times a day without even thinking about it. It is the part of the brain that enables you to walk, run, and drive a car with little or no effort. Our kids now ride their bikes effortlessly. They "Just Do It."

We are very excited about the **life changing process** we are about to initiate together. As a result of combining the MindScan with the guidance of this Off-Season Playbook, we are about to experience a new and dynamic interpersonal relationship. Above all else, we value the trust you have placed in us as a facilitator(s). We honor your decision to allow us to help you accelerate your journey of personal development.

Thank you for your confidence. We promise you a most enriching experience.

Very truly yours,

Walter Bond
Rich Campe
and the entire ProAdvisor Coach team

The Off-Season for Financial Advisors

The essentials for every Off-Season that your coach better be telling YOU!

ALL Games are won or lost based on the Off-Season.

Professional athletes and business leaders know that winning is about planning, preparation and execution. So often Advisors find themselves working "IN" the business the majority of the time and not finding the time to work "ON" the business. This Off-Season playbook will help you harness the best within yourself to re-discover your natural ability and achieve new heights both personally and professionally. As coaches we can narrow this down into two primary questions to quickly discover if you are running your business or if you business is running you.

Do you have an Off-Season (time to work on your business)?

Do you have a plan for your Off-Season (what to do with your Off-Season time)?

If you answered "No" to either of the questions above you are like the majority of Financial Advisors who find themselves not becoming all they can become by truly leveraging themselves and their business to have more time, money and fun. Hold onto your seat... this is a ride that will change your life and business forever. Take a deep breath and enjoy the discovery of a big bold future!

This book is dedicated to our families who endured countless hours of research, time and energy to make this book a reality. Thank you for your patience.

The following essentials for the Advisor Off-Season are based on the research from ProAdvisor Coach and the thousands of Financial Advisors, Insurance Agents, Managers and Top Producers.

We would like to acknowledge several key Master Coaches and industry leaders who have helped make this Off-Season Playbook possible...

Master Coach Todd Mauney, Founding Partner and President of ProAdvisor Coach – His passion to empower professionals to achieve their best and countless hours developing much of the content has made this book possible.

Master Coach Machen MacDonald, CPCC, CSCC – His financial services industry expertise and commitment to bringing coaching into this industry have been invaluable.

Master Coach Mark Sheer, Mark has been instrumental in his pursuit of the ideal client's model and serving the financial services industry.

Brian Chapman and Bill Friess, Regional Vice President's with Woodbury Financial. Brian and Bill are key leaders who helped to define the core elements of the most successful Financial Advisors.

Jamie Croland, CFP – Wholesaler with Planco – Jamie truly believes in adding value to the Advisors he works with and has played a key role in harnessing the best from everyone he partners with.

Jon Massey, Producer and CEO of The Massey Group – Thanks for your continued commitment to always growing and pursuing your creative dream.

Mark Johnson, CWC, CMFC, RHU – Producer and partner with Bauer, Captain and Johnson – Thank you for never giving up on yourself or others.

Scott Meyerson, AAMS, Top Advisor with Edward Jones – Thank you for believing in us and coaching. You are the ultimate example of stepping up and achieving results at a whole new level.

Jim Lake, The Guardian – Sr. Vice President – Thanks for your "Big Bold Vision" to always take it to the next level. You have transformed the industry with your creative ability to think "Out of the Box" regarding leadership and people performance.

Doyle Williams, Chief Marketing Officer with Country Financial – Thanks for believing and testing the model first hand.

Julian Good, CLU, ChFC – MDRT President 2011 – Thanks for being a constant student of life and business. Your leadership, dedication and commitment have impacted countless lives.

John Passananti, Executive Vice President, AXA Equitable Chicago - Thanks for all your clarity, endurance and strength. Your perseverance is an example for all leaders to model.

Contents

Chapter One

Awareness... It All Starts With You!

The Off-Season Peak Performance Best Practices Ever

When we set out to create the Off-Season Program, our goals were to create a coaching track specifically for financial professionals that would be 100% structured to ensure duplicatable success with 100% flexibility to meet the unique needs of each client.

First, we learned from the successes and failures of the top producers, leaders and best coaches in the financial space, handpicking only the best programs, tools and content.

Second, we structured the content as interactive exercises where accountability is an essential ingredient for success so you can have more time, money and fun. In total, the Off-Season Playbook is comprised of 22 metrics-based activities specifically designed to accelerate results... personally and professionally over a 7 week period of time followed by the measurable accountability, action and achievement required to provide a return on your investment.

The Off-Season Playbook utilizes four different accountability action tracking reviews:

1. MAP - Momentum Action Plan (reviewed quarterly)

2. KPIs (Key Performance Indicators) (reviewed weekly)

3. Strategies (reviewed daily)

4. Projects and Daily Metrics (reviewed weekly)

For the purposes of setting the foundation for a great "Off-Season" we will outline the most crucial foundational pieces for the best "Off-Season" yet so you can get the highest return on your time and money invested. As I'm sure you're aware, many sport teams take off 3 or more months to plan, review films, adjust plays, do drills and master the key elements necessary to execute and win games during the "In Season". Because we realize it may be difficult for you to take 3 months off to really have a full "Off-Season" to plan... this program is set up for you to complete over a 7 week period of time (about 3 hours per week).

Before you get started we would recommend carving out 3 hours per week on your calendar to work on your business and ensure you have an amazing "Off-Season" with an even better "In Season". The 7 week program is 100% scripted and 100% flexible so if you feel the need to move faster or slower that's up to you; however, based on momentum experience, we would highly encourage you to complete the program in 7 weeks or less to experience the best results.

Getting Started:

Objectives	Action Item(s)
Goal for Week 1: To be familiar with the benefits, process, content and resources of this program. All the information is contained within this book and playbook. IF YOU HAVE NOT taken the MindScan, please take the assessment before getting started. The link to find the MindScan is located via the following link: www.ProAdvisorCoach.com/off-season *(NOTE: You will want to retake the MindScan every 90-120 days of coaching to measure shifts in your thinking patterns. You may also use this link with your team as part of week 1)*	**Action:** Review the playbook to gain a perspective for the information, content and resources available. ☐ Complete the on-line "MindScan" ☐ Call to schedule your "MindScan Review" ☐ Review your full MindScan with a ProAdvisor Coach for further discussion - (Included at no charge as part of this Off-Season Program) ☐ Complete your "Success Questionnaire" ☐ Complete "Coaching Readiness" ☐ Complete "Sweet Spot Analysis" ☐ Complete "Core Disciplines"

ProAdvisor Coach "Peak Performance through Self-Awareness - MAP - (Momentum Action Plan) for Accelerated Success" overview:

1) Structure

- MindScan Review

- 7 Weeks of Off-Season (3 hours per week) - Working "ON" your business not "IN" your business

- Carve out quiet time to read the Off-Season Playbook and complete the playbook exercises

- We encourage everyone to have a Professional Coach because it's often difficult to see the forest through the trees; however, if you don't have a Professional Coach at a minimum we would recommend having an outsider review your information and give you feedback. Your manager, Associate or Business partner may serve this purpose.

- Progressive learning process that creates structure and the agenda for each week

- 100% coaching flexibility to win those immediate opportunities and challenges. While going through the exercises you will notice immediate shifts in your thinking and actions.

- Action Items clarified and committed to from each week to build out your "Momentum Action Plan" (aka "MAP")

2) ProAdvisor Coach Deliverables &/or Resources

- MindScan™ assessment for self-awareness and mastery

- Momentum Action Plan ("MAP") & resources

- Sweet spot analysis

- Ideal client profile to increase efficiency

- Ideal client calculator

- Sales pipeline report
- Ideal week schedule
- Client review agenda
- Favorable introduction script

3) Coaching Expectations of Participants

- The DESIRE to grow and achieve more, personally and professionally
- The BELIEF that you have untapped potential within your grasp
- The WILLINGNESS to learn and take new action.

4) ProAdvisor Coach Targeted Results

- Increased prospecting efficiency (more qualified leads at lower cost)
- Increase closing efficiencies (more closes with less effort)
- Increase retention and additional business opportunities (more revenues from fewer clients over longer periods of time)
- More time, money and fun!

Playbook Exercise 1 - The MindScan (see p. 61)

Let's start in the beginning... with our thinking.

The MindScan is an invaluable tool for the two of us and hundreds of thousands of others over the last 50 years. We have utilized the MindScan with over 10,000 Financial Advisors to learn the most common patterns of thinking within the financial services industry. Specifically, what type of thinking makes up the most successful Advisors? Not just financial success but overall success and happiness.

The MindScan is based on over 140 years of research in the area of "Axiology" and most recently in the last 50 years based on "Formal Axiology". Axiology refers to the science of values, while formal axiology refers to the mathematical measurement of values. What makes the MindScan stand out and be different from all other assessment tools is that it measures thinking at a mathematical level and not a personality level. A personality test compares you to other people; however, the MindScan doesn't compare you to anyone because it's based on mathematics. What this means is we can measure thinking today, gain awareness, make intentional decisions and adjust our thinking. Much like "IQ" measures our "Intellectual Quotient" the MindScan measures our "TQ" or "Thinking Quotient".

What we have found while working with thousands of Financial Advisors is that many know what to do yet they don't do it. Why? Because we are not starting at the beginning with our thinking. Much like an iceberg only reveals about 20% of the total iceberg above the water with the other 80% being hidden under the water. What sank the Titanic? What we could see or what we couldn't see? It was what we couldn't see under the water. The same thing is true in our business and life in that we need to be consciously aware of our thinking "under the water line". The MindScan is very easy to take by ranking two sets of 18 statements from best to worst. It should take you 20 minutes or less to complete. We would also encourage you to take advantage of the MindScan review which will take about 40 minutes.

Information on taking the MindScan and having a MindScan coach review session can be found at www.ProAdvisorCoach.com/offseason , by phone call ProAdvisor Coach at 704-752-7760 or email at info@ProAdvisorCoach.com.

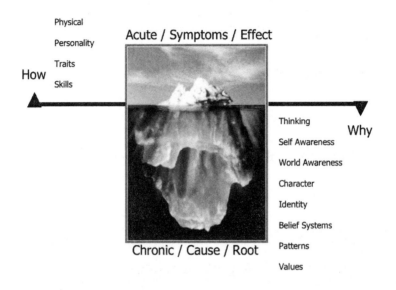

We can still remember a friend that lost $35,000 because he didn't understand his thinking. In fact, we could go as far to say that all success or failure can be directly tied back to our thinking. Think about it... what do we do without thinking? The reality is we have between 45,000 and 65,000 thoughts per day and 90% of the thoughts we have are patterns of thinking from the previous day. Even more amazing is until now we never had a way to mathematically understand our patterns of thinking.

Back to our friend that lost $35,000 of other people's money because he didn't understand his thinking. Just out of college our friend was ready to go by starting his own business at age 21. He raised $35,000 from friends and family to start his new endeavor. He had set some lofty goals while feeling confident he could become profitable. He committed to have all the investor money back to them within 45 days. After 40 days of selling he had spent the $35,000 and only sold $600 worth of services.

Because our friend did not understand his own thinking he was not able to see "under the waterline" and avoid losing $35,000. Much like we have three primary colors that make up all color the same thing is true with our thinking. Thinking can be boiled down into three primary dimensions called "The Relater", "The Doer" and "The Thinker".

The Relater is all about people, relationships and our ability to understand and connect with people well.

The Doer is all about taking action and seeing all the ways to get something done.

The Thinker is all about planning, process and structure.

Because our friend was overvaluing the Relater and the Doer he was able to raise the money from his connections and ability to think quickly on his feet; however, because our friend highly undervalued the importance of the Thinker he failed to have a realistic plan. We can walk all day long with massive action looking for a sunset headed east to never find the sunset. Great action without the realistic view of reality is a recipe for failure.

What if you had a way to see your natural pattern of thinking and avoid obstacles along the way? Better yet, what if you could understand your thinking so well that you could leverage your natural thinking strengths and manage your potential thinking weaknesses? Now you can and it's called the MindScan.

Playbook Exercise 2 - Success Questionnaire (see p. 70)

"Clarity and Focus are key elements of all success."

Before we go any further be sure to take your MindScan and review your results. Take notes, highlight, underline and let some others that know you personally review your MindScan with you. You should have a good idea at this point regarding your natural areas of thinking and capacities based on "the largest circles". You should also have a strong feel for your areas of attention based on the "location of circles" on the bias scale. If you still need some time to learn about your thinking please do that now before proceeding.

This next tool was created to help understand what success looks like for you. The Success Questionnaire is like a great detective uncovering parts of the puzzle to reveal the true wonder within each of us. The answers are in the questions and we would encourage you to play full out in answering all the questions to reveal your vision of success. Depending on your MindScan results defining success will be easy or extremely difficult; however, it's important to define what success looks like so we can tie this together with your overall purpose, passion and profit so you can have more time, money and fun.

We remember a time working with a client by the name of Sarah. She was earning about $150,000 per year and had been working in the financial services space for 12 years. Her biggest income year ever was $157,000 but she just couldn't take her business to the next level consistently. While filling out the success questionnaire she discovered that she had several people she felt were very successful both personally and financially. In addition, she realized that she had a high motivation for increasing her health and vitality along with her spiritual purpose yet she felt lost and not motivated to take the action necessary to achieve the results. Sarah also realized that she was consistently beating herself up and using negative words to describe herself. Statements like "I'm fat", I'm exhausted", "I don't have any time", "I'm not sure I can ever achieve my dreams" and "What's the point?". After learning about a few people Sarah considered to be successful

9

and defining some of her goals, she was able to define what she really wanted and what success looked like for her.

Sarah now defines success like this...

- Living a life full of health and vitality

- Weighing 142 pounds

- Running and working out 3 - 4 days per week

- Being connected with my creator and my purpose by reading the Bible in a year

- Earning $250,000 per year

- Enjoying my free time with my family

- Travel 3 weeks per year

- Taking off Fridays

This was a HUGE step for Sarah in getting clear about her future and what success looked like for her. She then felt like a weight was lifted off her shoulders and she had a new success vision of the future that would help pull her into the next phase of her life journey.

Most people never take the "Off-Season" time to define what success looks like and therefore they end up reacting to the urgency of each day instead of charging forward with a compelling, bright and exciting vision of success.

Playbook Exercise 3 - Coaching Readiness (see p. 76)

"When the student is ready the teacher will appear."

The above quote is all about the coachability index or coach readiness. Are you ready to be coached? What this really means is are you really ready to take your life and business to the next level? It's like having a cup that's full of water "dead water". When the cup is full we can't put anymore water in; however, if we pour out some water we can add more "living water" to the cup. Is your cup so full that you can't take in any new "living water"? In many cases those who need coaching the most also resist coaching the most and so they remain in the same old pattern year after year. Top Advisors recognize that ALL top athletes and Business Leaders have coaches.

The fact is that only 10% or less of the Advisors that purchased this Playbook have even opened the book. If you are currently reading this then "congratulations" because you are part of the select few that "do" versus those who "don't" and you're doing GREAT! The truth is... Successful people can become complacent with success and then they stop growing both personally and professionally and wonder why they don't feel successful anymore. The reality is...the positive feelings we have are usually when we're growing, achieving and becoming all we can become. Think about a time when you were achieving all types of goals, very motivated and driven for success. How did you feel? Alive, rejuvenated, accomplished, successful? That's because we have a drive deep within all of us to become all of who we can be.

The Coaching Readiness will give you a gauge of how coachable you are currently. Do you still invest in yourself? Do you still take the time to read, learn and grow? Are you still open to constructive feedback? Do you share your successes with your team? After you complete the Coaching Readiness please share with your coach, manager, associate or someone close to get feedback.

Before we can assess your readiness for coaching, we need to be clear on what coaching is and isn't.

Nicki Keohohou - (Speaker, Author and Coach for direct sales) describes coaching as a bridge...it's a bridge that can help us go from where we are now to where we want to be, and really enjoy the journey.

Coaching is not...

- Handholding (creating dependency)

- Caretaking (coddling and enabling)

- Consulting (providing all the answers)

- Implementation (doing the work for you)

- Mentoring (teaching you to follow his/her way of doing things)

Dr. Howard Hendricks - (Long Time Professor at Dallas Theological Seminary and Speaker for Promise Keepers) stated it quite well..."Coaching is a hands-on process designed to enable people to LEARN, DEVELOP and ultimately IMPROVE performance through greater COMPETENCE AND CONFIDENCE."

The Professional Coach Is...

- A champion to help you turn things around

- A sounding board for processing and decision making

- An encourager and supporter in times of adversity and challenge

- A co-creator in the development of "BHAG" (Big Hairy Audacious Goals)

- A light in dark and rough times

- A wake-up call for times when you need it

- A trainer in thinking, communication and life skills

- A motivator when action is required

- A partner in achieving your life's dreams, goals and abundance

- A coach helps others DEVELOP and GROW, something we MUST do all our lives in order to truly THRIVE

Are you ready to embrace coaching, develop and grow in order to discover the best of whom you are and achieve your true purpose? Well, let's see…

Do you believe more is possible in your life and that you have the potential to do more right now? If you are going to succeed you will have to condition yourself to succeed, every day! The aim of the program is to have you develop and condition beliefs, thinking and patterns that will help you to succeed for the rest of your life!

Playbook Exercise 4 - Sweet Spot Analysis (see p. 78)

In every sport we have what we call Sweet Spot(s). A place that everything aligns perfectly and a sweet spot is created. It's the perfect stroke in golf where the ball hits the club head exactly right and you feel as if the swing was effortless as your ball flies straight down the center of the fairway. In tennis it's the perfect spot on the racquet that causes the tennis ball to respond with the least amount of effort and the best possible result.

A "Sweet Spot Analysis" is used to identify the most beneficial places for you to be spending your time with the highest reward; however, it's also a place that's effortless with passionate energy. We look at the sweet spot as being the combination of three critical elements to include your passion, purpose and profit. Your passion refers to your place of excitement and joy. Your purpose refers to areas where you're naturally gifted and it's effortless for you to spend time achieving amazing results. Profit is the place you generate the most revenue as a return on time spent in that particular area. Some sweet spots may include spending time with... your ideal clients, centers of influence, strategic alliance partnerships, working on your business, managing your team, preparing cases, follow up calls, etc.

What we have found to be true time and time again is that top producers spend 80% or more of their time in no more than 3 sweet spots. Once you clearly identify your sweet spots as specifically as you can it's important to start measuring your time in your sweet spots. As you move closer and closer to the 80% plus of your time in your sweet spots you will find yourself having more Time, Money and Fun!!!

When Steve first approached us he was tired of being consumed by the long hours with no time for his family, friends and himself. Like most Advisors who run a business he was caught up in the urgent or reactive parts of his business and finding himself totally exhausted every day as if he was the gerbil on the never ending hamster wheel. After completing the "Sweet Spot Analysis" we quickly realized he had three "Sweet Spots".

1. Spending time with his 42 Ideal clients.

2. Spending time with his 4 Ideal Strategic Alliance Partners.

3. Spending time with his 7 Centers of Influence.

After we clearly defined Steve's Sweet Spots we learned that he was spending only 23% of his time in his Sweet Spots. We then asked Steve if he were able to spend 80% or more of his time in his three Sweet Spots what would that mean in terms of time, money and fun? Steve said "I would have 8 hours minimum per week of extra time to spend with my family and on the golf course. On a conservative level I would add $200,000 of additional profit per year to my bottom line and I would have a lot more fun." This is the reality for many Advisors and the obvious question is what do we do about it? The first step is creating this clarity of awareness by understanding what your Sweet Spots are and how much time you currently spend in your Sweet Spots. Next we need to be intentional about spending more time within the important Sweet Spots while tracking the progress over time. This will be outlined more clearly when we start laying out your MAP - Momentum Action Plan in Chapters 3 and 4.

Playbook Exercise 5 - Core Disciplines (see p. 82)

The core disciplines will help you get a 360 degree view of your entire practice. We have outlined the most critical 14 core areas of any successful financial services firm to help you hone in on the most critical areas for you. Use this tool as a base line awareness to fuel your success. The core disciplines will be very helpful over time as you can turn to them time and time again to illustrate your improvements.

Let's take a look at Jim and his Core Disciplines. Jim has been in the Financial Services industry for 21 years and he currently earns an average of $260,000 per year. When Jim first started working with us he felt like he was doing very well but knew he could be doing so much better. After filling out his Core Disciplines he realized he was doing very well in 9 of the 14 Core Disciplines; however, he realized he was lacking in 6 core areas that would make a huge difference in his business.

1. Understanding and defining his Ideal Clients he ranked himself a 3 on a 10 point scale and said he could improve this area by spending more time with his ideal clients to really understand them better. In addition he did some research and surveys of his ideal clients

2. Seeing enough ideal prospects he ranked himself a 2 on a 10 point scale and said he was not seeing enough new ideal prospects. He said he was getting a fair amount of referrals but they were not the right ideal client referrals. To improve in this area he said he could put a process in place to attract more ideal prospects and work with his Strategic Alliance partners and Centers of Influence more.

3. Target Marketing to his Ideal Clients he ranked himself a 0 on a 10 point scale and said he really never put a branding strategy in place. To improve in this area he said he would invest the time and money in defining his brand and putting

a branding plan in place to cover his web site, collateral and image to his ideal clients.

4. <u>Unique Value Offering</u> he ranked himself a 2 on a 10 point scale and said he felt like he was somewhat unique and also felt like every other Advisor on the market. Jim said he would spend the time to really understand what differentiates his company from all the other Advisors in the market. He already starting thinking about what his Ideal Clients are saying about him like... he cares more than the other Advisors, he has great follow up and really understands what Doctors like me deal with on a regular basis regarding insurance companies, disability insurance and exit strategies.

5. <u>Marketing and Sales Process</u> he ranked himself a 3 on a 10 point scale and said he could put a sales funnel in place to accurately track the flow of referrals, new appointments, closed appointments and closes so he can avoid the roller coaster ride of up and down sales and revenue.

Once we gathered the information from the Core Disciplines we could develop a plan of action to move forward. Again, the first step is always creating the awareness coupled with the intention to move forward. We will outline action steps and a plan in Chapters 3 and 4 as part of the MAP - Momentum Action Plan.

Chapter Two

Your Ideal Clients

The Key to your business plan

Objectives	Action Item(s)
Goal for Week 2: Set positive foundation for discovery, learning and achievement.	**Action (for review on week 2):**
Key Topics:	□ Complete "<u>Call Maximizer</u>"
□ Introductions and orientation □ MindScan review □ Business strengths and potential weaknesses □ Advisor core disciplines	□ Run MindScan on 3 significant relationships □ Complete "<u>Ideal Client Profile</u>" □ Complete any Incompletes

Note: Read you MindScan and have 2 other people close to you read your MindScan. Underline, highlight and take notes.

PAC "Peak Performance through Self-Awareness - MAP for Accelerated Success": Week 2

Objectives: Bruce Tuckman, a respected educational psychologist and bestselling author who first described the four stages of all group development for high performance teams that starts with "forming" as setting the crucial foundation for 'getting real' where discovery and accountability take place. Our goal for Chapter 2 is to set the right foundation for maximum discovery, learning and achievement through the process. Discovery begins immediately with a focus on the "Success Cycle" of thinking and what the MindScan thinking assessment reveals around thinking strengths and potential weaknesses. As we move through the process, this awareness will be coached to intention where new habits will form that improve our business results.

Specifically, Advisors will walk away with:

- An awareness of how to leverage your thinking to get the most from your Off-Season and your business.

- An awareness of your greatest thinking strength(s) and how to leverage them to improve results.

- An awareness of their greatest potential thinking weakness(s) and how to prevent them from hindering achievement.

- An understanding of the "Success Cycle" pattern of thinking, your current pattern of thinking and specific strategies to shift thinking and break limiting cycle.

- Knowing how important it is to be aware of your "sweet spot" and creating a plan that allows you to spend more time on those activities.

- Greater appreciation for diverse thinking within your teams and how to better leverage the diversity and create more synergy for greater achievement.

- An overview of critical best practices within your business and the importance of 'grading' your business against these best practices to identify the critical gaps.

Playbook Exercise 6 - Coaching Maximizer (see p. 95)

The Coaching Maximizer is designed to be a weekly tool to keep the momentum and track your progress. Use this with your coach, mentor, manager or associate to assist you in keeping the course.

Playbook Exercise 7 - MindScan's
on 3 significant relationships (see p. 99)

Now that you have a better understanding of thinking and how it works with you it's time to understand your team. Take the time to run a MindScan on 3 significant relationships to learn how you can best work together in achieving your vision. What we have found is that any conflict that may arise is simply a mismatch of value. The Mind-Scan link can be found at www.ProAdvisor Coach.com/offseason

As an example you may find yourself valuing results as the most important value while someone else on your team may find that people are the most important. This will cause a rub for you and your team without knowing the cause of the friction or conflict.

We can still remember working with Joe and his Administrative assistant Patricia. While Joe was very committed to his goals and structure to achieve the goals set, his assistant Patricia valued people with very high attentiveness. Every time a phone call would come into the office for Joe, Patricia would expect Joe to take the call immediately while Joe felt like he was being interrupted from the priorities at hand and Patricia felt disregarded because Joe would not take the call immediately. This created major conflict within the office because neither Joe nor Patricia understood the importance of each other's values.

Once they both took the MindScan and understood each other's values they could work in harmony around the shared values while leveraging each other's natural strengths and managing each other's potential weaknesses. They resolved this by Joe understanding the importance of Patricia's value for people and Patricia understanding Joe's importance for action and systems. Now when a call comes in Patricia takes care of the majority of the calls herself by adding that special caring touch while scheduling any other calls on Joe's calendar for future follow up. In this example both feel valued, they serve the clients better and they work in harmony to achieve the vision for the organization.

Playbook Exercise 8 - Ideal Client Profile (see p. 100)

Ideal clients are the life blood of any successful Advisor business. In most cases about 10% - 20% of our entire client base is made up of Ideal Clients. The questions are:

- Do we have our Ideal Clients defined?

- Do we know who our Ideal Clients currently are?

- Do we spend the time to nurture and develop our Ideal Clients?

- How do we get more Ideal Clients?

We asked Mark Sheer to assist us with the Ideal clients and Favorable Introductions. Mark is a ProAdvisor Master Coach with a specialty focus around Ideal Clients and Favorable Introductions

Master Coach Mark said "I remember very clearly about 16 years ago when I first began coaching in the financial services community a conversation I had with Tucker, a top producer. We were discussing referrals and Tucker said he did not need more referrals, what he wanted was qualified introductions. He said that 80% of his referrals were not qualified and therefore did not produce the results he was seeking. He wanted more of his top 20% or "A" clients to introduce him to people just like them—actual potential clients. He thought that 80% of the referrals or names that his clients gave him were of no more value than a cold call.

So I asked Tucker to work with me and focus on what his top 20% looked like. What unique characteristics would his Ideal Client embody? Together we comprised a list that included both psychographics, i.e., someone who is a helper, is fun and easy to get along with, cares about their family and their financial well being. We also determined that this Ideal Client would be someone who would listen to his advice and have the ability to implement the recommendations he made. And we established that his Ideal client should have very specific demographics, i.e., certain levels of income, investible assets, net worth, age range and be located near his office.

I then asked Tucker what type of visual aid or tool he was using to effectively communicate to his existing qualified or "A" clients and centers of influence what he is looking for in an Ideal Client.

Tucker said that he was standing in front of the client when he spoke to them and *he* was the visual aid. We laughed and I shared with him that 80% of us are visually dominant and if he would show them a written Ideal Client Profile, with both psychographics and demographics he would get 80% qualified referrals which we could turn into favorable introductions—and the Ideal Client Profile was born.

Tucker experienced an immediate increase in both the quality and quantity of favorable introductions, as did other clients.

In the last 16 years our top students who effectively use our Get More "A" Clients system, which includes customizing your Ideal Profile, have found they get 1 or 2 new "A" clients per month."

Chapter Three

The MAP - "Momentum Action Plan" - Part I

Objectives	Action Item(s)
Goal for Week 3: Develop a 'MAP' (Momentum Action Plan) for your business from the top down...starting with a profile of your ideal client, defining your UVP (unique value proposition) and having a clear vision with a mission. **Key Topics:** ☐ Understanding target marketing and define "Ideal Client." ☐ Understanding the importance of Vision and defining yours. ☐ Understanding the importance of Mission and define yours. ☐ Aligning Vision, Mission and KPIs (Key Performance Indicators) within your business.	**Action (for review on week 3):** ☐ Complete "Call Maximizer" ☐ Complete 'Vision' in "Vision/Mission/Values" ☐ Complete 'Mission' in "Vision/Mission/Values" ☐ Complete 'Values' in "Vision/Mission/Values"

PAC "Peak Performance through Self-Awareness - MAP for Accelerated Success": Week 3

Objectives: Having an acute awareness of your target market, their critical needs and the businesses 'unique value proposition' to satisfy those needs better than anyone else are fundamentals of business often overlooked or minimized in planning. Michael Gerber in his book "The e-Myth Revisited" talks about the distinction between working "IN" vs. working "ON" the business. You can't have one without the other but most business owners embrace their roles as technicians working most of the time "IN" their business rather than "ON" it. Working on your business is your "Off-Season"

This chapter explains the difference and emphasizes the importance of balancing both and time management. The most important "Off-Season" activity is planning and a sound action/business plan should always begin with a clear target market, their critical needs and your company's unique value proposition for satisfying those needs.

Specifically, you will achieve:

- The value of an action/business plan, the critical components of it and how to manage the plan for implementation and maximum results.

- A clear understanding why having an "ideal client profile" is foundational for a business plan.

- The tools and skills needed to create an "ideal client profile", identify their critical needs, design a "unique value proposition" to satisfy those needs and brand it for competitive advantage.

- An understanding of what "vision" and "mission" are, their purpose in a plan and how to create them based on the above.

- The importance of "vision casting" within and outside the business as part of a powerful branding and positioning strategy. We will also discuss the importance of an "elevator statement" and how to create one.

Playbook Exercise 9 - Coaching Maximizer (see p. 107)

Keep going with your Coaching Maximizer. You should start to see some patterns and some areas for development.

Playbook Exercise 10 and 11 - Vision and Mission (see p. 111)

Motivation on Steroids: The Power of Vision

"Without Vision, the People Perish." Proverbs 29:18

What does this quote mean? Ever wondered what the 'giants' of human kind have in common? You guessed it, a VISION (Visual Image of Success In Our Neurology). Our neurological system is what creates thinking and action. When we imagine with our minds it excites the emotions which creates the energy we need to overcome obstacles, achieve dreams and create more abundance in the world!

Countless leadership and personal development gurus agree on the importance of having a personal vision for your life. Warren Bennis, Stephen Covey, Peter Senge, and others point out that a powerful vision can help you succeed far beyond where you'd be without one. That vision can propel you and inspire those around you to reach their own dreams. Without a vision, others will plan and direct your life for you which leads to resentment, regret, guilt and pain.

Vision inspires the HOPE of an ABUNDANT future. The opposite of abundance is scarcity. Do you know anyone that lives in scarcity? Sure...in fact we've all experienced it at some point. It's most evident when we see and verbalize what's wrong with our lives and the world around us, how little money there is, faults of others, intolerance, who's doing them wrong and the like. It's focusing on what's lacking in the world instead of the plentiful side. Are you living in abundance or scarcity? Careful, you may feel abundance on the surface when scarcity is looming below.

Vision & Mission - What's The Difference?

A *Vision statement*: describes what you want to become at some point in the future; it's the 'picture' of the ideal future.

A *Mission statement*: describes you today, concentrating on the present. It describes your customer(s), critical processes and establishes performance targets.

These statements are often confused. At the core of your Vision is your identity and what you and your future will look like. Your Mission says why it exists and how you will live out your identity and move towards the realization of your vision. The Vision describes a future while Mission describes how you're self actualizing it today. A Mission statement defines the purpose, the broader reason for existing and being in business. It serves as an ongoing operating guide based on values. The mission can remain the same for decades if crafted well. Vision is more specific in terms of objective and a future state. Vision is related to some form of achievement if successful.

Features of an effective vision statement may include:

- Clear and lacking ambiguity

- Invokes imagination and pictures of "what it will look and be like"

- It's excites and stimulates emotion

- Memorable and captivating...has a "Wow" factor

- Seems barely achievable and realistic

- Congruent with values

- It attracts certain people and repels others

- It emboldens, inspires and galvanizes the ones sharing the vision

Clearly articulating your vision, mission and values are critically important for several reasons:

- Source of inspiration

- Plum line and criteria for decision making

- It's motivating to know you're living on purpose and with intention

- It creates an air of confidence

- It provides an overriding sense of direction, especially when you get off track

- It's liberating because you know what to say "yes" and *"NO"* to

- It's a plumb line for all other goals and dreams

- It provides synergy in your life connecting all the 'dots'

- It empowers you to live into your strengths rather than be something you are not

- It connects you to a higher power, knowing that you were created with a purpose

Which comes first? The mission statement or the vision statement? That depends. If you have a new start up business, new program or plan to re-engineer your current services, then the vision will guide the mission statement and the rest of the strategic plan. If you have an established business where the mission is established, then many times, the mission can serve as window through which you may see your ultimate vision. Either way, you need to know where you are, your current resources, your current obstacles, and where you want to go - the vision for the future.

In order to become really effective, a vision statement must become assimilated into your personal and professional life. In whatever role you have as a leader, father, mother, business owner and the like, you have the responsibility of casting the vision regularly, creating narratives that illustrate the vision and acting as a role-model by embodying the vision which can change lives and the world!

There's no "magic" formula for coming up with your life vision and mission. It's a discovery process that must be approached with some intention, intuition, patience and perseverance. This exercise is designed to focus your mind on the "clues" that will likely give you the answers you need. You may begin with a few statements that seem a bit fuzzy at first but be patient. Over time, hours, weeks, perhaps even months, it will evolve and become clearer to you as you focus your subconscious and it begins to pick up more clues from life without you even knowing it. Because this is a process of discovery, we recommend you go through this exercise once a year to see how the picture is getting clearer. Enjoy the journey!

Playbook Exercise 12 - Values (see p. 111)

Values drive our behaviors that drive our actions that drive our results.

It's important to become aware of your values so you can align your values within your daily life, business and plan.

We specifically remember a coaching call with Mike because he was really frustrated. His values were crossed and not aligned. He really loved all his clients and he really wanted to grow his business. He felt like he couldn't stop taking care of all his clients and yet at the same time he just didn't have enough time to grow his business because of all the clients he had to serve. He was in a catch 22... darned if he grows because he felt he had to stop serving his existing clients and darned if he doesn't grow his business because he felt like he needed to provide for himself and his family more.

Once Mike realized that he could serve his existing clients even better while growing his business his whole world opened up and he had a new peace of mind. In fact, Mike was able to leverage his values to gain huge momentum in achieving both his goals of growing the business and serving his clients. We achieved this by aligning values through questions. Everything changed when this question was asked... How are you letting down your clients by not growing your business? He stopped and thought for a moment and then realized that because he was not growing he could not afford all the new technology, staff and resources he wanted to put in place to really create a raving customer experience and that by not generating more income to serve his clients more he was actually hurting them. This was a big "Ah Ha" moment for Mike and he quickly started creating a plan for growing the business while serving his clients in amazing new ways. It was like the handcuffs came off and he was free to think and become all he was meant to become.

Chapter Four

The Map "Momentum Action Plan" - Part II

Objectives	Action Item(s)
Goal for Week 4: Defining your "North" on the compass with clear KPIs (Key Performance Indicators) to focus your resources and energies where YOU determine they will yield the highest ROI (Return On Investment). Creating TOM (Top Of Mind) awareness of your most critical relationships, starting with those in your sales funnel and on your ideal client list. **Key Topics:** ☐ The value of and defining KPIs (Key Performance Indicators). ☐ The value of and defining Strategies. ☐ Client segmentation strategies (identifying your most 'ideal clients'). ☐ TOM (Top Of Mind) awareness of your sales pipeline.	**Action (for review on week 4):** ☐ Complete "Call Maximizer" ☐ Complete "Activity Planner" for KPIs and Strategies ☐ Segment and List your existing "Ideal Clients" ☐ Complete Sales Funnel tab in Critical Relationship Tracker [Excel file download]

PAC "Peak Performance through Self-Awareness - MAP for Accelerated Success": Week 4

Objectives: This week models the balance between working "ON" and working "IN" activities. In working "ON" the business, we continue to build the action/business plan defining their KPIs (Key Performance Indicators) and listing different strategies for achieving those metrics, both based on industry best practices. The working "IN" component will be to define a process for segmenting your existing clients and immediately implementing it while compiling all 'open' sales opportunities into a "Sales Pipeline Report" so they can be managed more effectively, proactively and with a greater sense of urgency.

Specifically, you will walk away with:

- A clear definition of what a KPI is and how to create the right KPIs for your business.

- Examples of best practice KPIs from successful firms.

- Methods for creating alignment between the firm's KPIs and individual roles within the team.

- A segmentation strategy that will work for you and a process for achieving it.

- Renewed appreciation for the value of managing a "sales pipeline" report and specific tools to use.

- An understanding of how to use client segmentation strategies to increase leads, close more sales and retain clients longer with greater satisfaction.

Playbook Exercise 13 - Coaching Maximizer (see p. 119)

You're doing great! Keep up with your Call Maximizer. It would be helpful to let your coach or someone close to you review your progress to date.

Playbook Exercise 14 - Activity Planner (see p. 123)

The Activity Planner is used to capture the key elements for execution and achievement of your MAP. The Activity Planner includes 5 key elements included below...

1. Focus Areas - Key areas of focus both personally and in business. This may tie back to your value although it's not a must.

2. KPIs - Key Performance Indicators used to measure the Big Rocks or key elements of your plan. KPIs should be SMART - Specific, Measurable, Actionable, Realistic and Time bound.

3. Strategies - All the ideas you have to achieve your KPIs.

4. Projects - Specific projects you will put in place to achieve your KPIs.

5. Critical Activities - The daily, weekly or monthly activities needed to achieve your outcomes.

The Activity Planner is where the rubber meets the road. It's your living, breathing, action plan to move toward your Big Vision.

Matt is an Advisor earning $167,000 per year and he has been in the business for 16 years. After coaching Matt for a few weeks he had completed his Vision and Mission and he was ready for the Activity Planner. Based on Matt's Vision he wanted to increase his revenues from $221,000 per year to $400,000 per year, while taking Fridays off to spend more time with his family. His Activity Planner looked like this:

Focus Areas:

Business Growth

Operational Effectiveness

KPI's:

Increase revenue from $221,000 to $400,000 by December 24th 2010

Hire an office manager by June 1st of 2010

Strategies:

Ideal Client process in place

Segment Client base

Invest in a branding strategy

Re-Do Web site

Put favorable introduction process in place

Leverage online systems to post job descriptions

Send email to associates and friends regarding job posting

Projects:

5 New Ideal Clients by August 15, 2010

New Web Site in place by July 1, 2010

Hire new office manager position by August 15, 2010

Critical Activities:

- 5 New Ideal Clients by August 15, 2010
    - Order Mark Sheer Ideal client program at ProAdvisor site - 5/1/2010
    - Study material - 5/15/2010
    - Role play with Coach - 5/25/2010

- Segment Client base - 5/27/2010

- Contact Ideal existing clients to set 7 appointments - 6/1/2010

- Coach Ideal Clients on Favorable Intros - 6/15/2010

- New Web Site in place by July 1, 2010

  - Get recommendations for Advisors on best firms - 5/1/2010

  - Contact firms and get demo of top 3 - 5/15/2010

  - Decide on final development firm - 5/25/2010

  - Start work on web site - 6/10/2010

- Hire new office manager position by August 15, 2010

  - Get job description from Manager and Coach - 5/1/2010

  - Review job description and make changes - 5/15/2010

  - Research sites for job descriptions - 5/15/2010

  - Post new job description - 5/21/2010

  - Review candidates weekly - 5/25/2010

  - Interview 2 per week starting - 6/1/2010

Once Matt had his MAP build out it was time to execute his plan to achieve his Vision for 2010 and we are happy to say that Matt exceeded his 2010 Vision by achieving $417,000 in revenue for 2010. Way to go Matt! Remember the MAP is meant to be alive, real and dynamic. Work with your coach, manager or leader to adjust and modify create a MAP that's unique to you and your dreams.

Playbook Exercise 15 - Ideal Clients (see p. 125)

Let's turn again to our specialty coach Mark Sheer to gain some additional clarity on our Ideal Clients and segmenting them.

Once you gain clarity on your Ideal Client Profile, it's critically important to focus on "Who To Ask" by segmenting your clients for maximum results.

Recently, I was working with Fred, an Advisor, who asked, "Whom should I ask or start with to get the best results?"

I asked Fred to write a list of three "A" clients who fit the following:

- You have a high-trust relationship with them.

- They are the helping type and would like to help people they care about as well as you.

- They are people of influence, meaning, if they suggest a friend, colleague, co-worker, business associate or center of influence to meet with you (their advisor) they most likely will meet with you because of the influence the person introducing you has in the relationship.

Fred thought for a few moments, smiled and started segmenting his list and writing down "A" clients who fit the high-trust, helper, influential profile categories.

We then practiced how best to approach these influential referral sources. When Fred contacted the first "A" client, the client favorably introduced Fred to seven qualified, potential clients of which the first two met with Fred right away. One became a fee-paying, financial-planning client and the second said they probably would become clients very soon.

So it's very important to segment your clients and centers of influence into your "A" - client list to maximize your effectiveness and results. If you ask the right people the process will almost always work. And remember to have your "A" clients also favorably introduce you to their Centers of Influence such as CPAs and Attorneys.

You will be pleasantly surprised how you can open many profitable doors and minds using this approach.

Playbook Exercise 16 - Sales Funnel (see p. 126)

A sales funnel is a foundational part of any successful business. By having a strong sales funnel in place we eliminate the roller coaster ride that most entrepreneurs face on a regular bases. The question is "are you running your business or is your business running you?" You should be able to turn your sales up or down depending on your intention much like turning the water up, down, off or on.

Let's take a look at our Advisor friend John. John has been an Advisor for 17 years and he was earning an average of $187,000 per year. John was experiencing what most advisors face on a regular basis... "the ups and downs of sales and revenue". Once we understood the key components of his sales funnel we could quickly focus on the most important areas of need.

Week: 6/1/2010

Appointments Scheduled:	9
Appointments Kept:	8
Cases Opened:	5
Cases Closed:	4
Revenue Closed:	$3,857
Qualified, Committed and Coachable Relationships scheduled:	0
New Favorable Introductions from QCC's:	0

In John's case he was great at closing sales; however, he was not good at setting appointments with his "Qualified, Committed and Coachable Ideal Clients" to get new favorable introductions. By having a clear sales funnel in place we could quickly understand the critical areas that needed focus. Together we modified two areas within his business.

We put a system in place for his assistant to set up new appointments on a regular basis with his ideal clients for reviews and new business.

We put a favorable introduction plan in place to generate new ideal clients.

Now John has a more consistent peace of mind because he knows at all times what type of revenue is coming in and he is better prepared for the future.

Chapter Five

The Time of Your Life

Objectives	Action Item(s)
Goal for Week 5: Break your KPIs down to quarterly objectives, focus on the next 90 days and execute with intention every day of the week. Success becomes a habit!	**Action (for review on week 5):**
	□ Complete "Call Maximizer"
Key Topics:	□ List Quarterly objectives in MAP
	□ Identify those due in 90 days
□ Working in 90-day windows... defining short-term goals and projects.	□ Create "Ideal Week" template
□ Maintaining focus, efficiency and accountability through the "Ideal Work Week" model	□ List and track "Critical Activities" with the "Activity Planner"
□ Tracking the critical weekly metrics...emphasis on New Client Leads	

PAC "Peak Performance through Self-Awareness - MAP for Accelerated Success": Week 5

Objectives: Having a plan is critical but implementing it is essential. Most advisors are so busy working "IN" the business, they may find it difficult to manage and implement a plan once they have it. This week puts the focus back on the fundamentals of proper time management techniques, working with 'time blocks' and defining the routine critical activities essential to their success.

Specifically, you will walk away with:

- An understanding of the importance of, how to focus on, how to define and how to manage 90-day goals and projects.

- A plan for creating a rhythm of accountability within your firm.

- The distinction between "lead" and "lag" indicators and how to manage them over time.

- Tools to create an "Ideal Week" to get more done, have more peace and operating more in your "sweet spot."

Playbook Exercise 17 - Coaching Maximizer (see p. 127)

Are you keeping up with you Coaching Maximizer? In the beginning this may seem like "do I have to?"; however, once you build this pattern you will see the benefits in time, money and fun.

Playbook Exercise 18 - Ideal Week (see p. 131)

Of all the tools, this one always sheds great light on the reality of time (our most valuable resource). We were working with a client by the name of Jake and he started the coaching with us because he had "No Time". He was volunteering as the President of a very large organization, married with 3 kids and trying desperately to take care of his health and business at the same time. Whenever we hear that someone has no time we quickly start looking at the facts by using the time tracker because when someone feels confined by time it's because they are reacting to time. They are not owning time or being intentional with their time. We have to be very intentional with our time because it's finite and we only have so much time each day. Everyone has the same 24 hours in a day. In Jake's case we used the time tracker to see the following and realized he actually had a bunch of time; however, he was not using his time wisely. Again, if you feel like you have "no time" the first step is to gather the facts. After you look at each week start to boil this down into big chucks of time. I'm always amazed at how much time we have compared to how much time we can't account for.

Jakes Hours by the Day, Week and Year:

	Day	Week	Year
Sleep	7	49	2548
Ideal Clients	3	21	1092
Family	2	14	728
Eat	2	14	728
Travel	3	21	1092
Volunteer	2	14	728
Total Time	**19**	**133**	**6916**
Total Available Time	**24**	**168**	**8736**
Unaccounted for Time	**5**	**35**	**1820**

In Jake's case we can't account for about 20% of his total time. That's about 76 days that are unaccounted for. This is calculated by dividing 1,820 unaccounted for hours in one year, divided by 24 hours in a day, equals 76 days that are unaccounted for per year. This is very common and very real. Now what to do with all the extra time? Again, the first step is to deal with the facts! If you are like most you are saying... "That's not true for me... I really have NO TIME".

What we can learn from Jake and countless others is that we might think we have no time; however, in the majority of situations we always have room for better utilization of our time, talent and resources. We have always found it fascinating to learn what Financial Advisors can do with their time and unfortunately most Advisors don't use the time to become all they can become. Take the time to understand the time of your life.

Playbook Exercise 19 - Activity Planner (see p. 140)

Based on your overall MAP from Playbook exercise 14 it's time to focus on some key parts to gain focus and momentum. What we have found from working with top Financial Advisors is that they have laser focus to sharpen in on the major areas. Start by identifying your Strategic Projects. You should have no more than 5 Strategic Projects you focus on at one time. Think about the areas that will impact your time, money and fun the most.

After you have the Strategic Projects identified it's time to move onto your Expected Results, Targeted Achievement Dates and Required Tasks.

While working with David, an Advisor with 17 years experience averaging $226,000 per year in income, we discovered he had an amazing detailed business plan but he lacked the execution of the plan. After identifying David's most important Strategic Projects, he was able to gain focus and momentum to execute his plan and achieve his vision.

Chapter Six

More Ideal Clients

Objectives	Action Item(s)
Goal for Week 6: Developing your Favorable Introduction strategy leveraging your ideal client relationships, alliance partners and centers of influence. This strategy alone could double your revenues! **Key Topics:** ☐ Introduction to the "Favorable Introduction" strategy ☐ Creating a client review agenda that leads to more Favorable Introductions ☐ Creating and using a Favorable Introduction script	**Action (for review on week 6):** ☐ Complete "Call Maximizer" ☐ Personalize the Client Review Agenda Template ☐ Personalize the Favorable Introduction Script ☐ Practice using the Client Review Agenda and Favorable Introduction Script with 4 people

PAC "Peak Performance through Self-Awareness - MAP for Accelerated Success": Week 6

Objectives: Having now profiled your "ideal clients", calculated the value of duplicating your "ideal clients" and creating an action/business plan to establish clear goals and a plan to achieve them, we now zero in on one of the most powerful strategies for expanding an advisor's sphere of influence and network...the "Favorable Introduction" strategy. We explain the difference between this strategy and simple "referrals" by identifying the three specific targets of this strategy...ideal clients, alliance partners and centers of influence. We will provide specific tools and instruction to implement this strategy immediately with existing clients and a weekly goal for new 'favorable introductions' to prospective clients, alliance partners and COIs.

Specifically, you will walk away with:

- A refreshing and empowering look at the distinction between a referral and a favorable introduction.

- Process, tools and instruction needed to get weekly favorable introductions.

- A 'big picture' appreciation for the power of this strategy in keeping the pipeline full, duplicating ideal clients and scaling the business over time.

Playbook Exercise 20 - Coaching Maximizer (see p. 147)

Way to go at keeping up with your Coaching Maximizer! You're in the final home stretch.

Playbook Exercise 21 -
Client Review Agenda Template (see p. 153)

We had a client by the name of Linda and she was explaining how each client was different to which we responded with "in what way?" Linda proceeded to explain "some clients want me to call them weekly, while others prefer I call them monthly, quarterly or not at all... some want email correspondence, others prefer face to face and others prefer connecting via the phone and some even said they prefer to connect via Text or Facebook".

We asked Linda if she had a Client Review Agenda for new clients and existing clients and she responded with "no". We used the template called Client Review Agenda located in the Off-Season Playbook to start the process. As we modified and created the agenda Linda started using it and felt much more in tune with her clients which in turn helped her to feel more at peace and relaxed. In addition, Linda was able to drive additional revenue in a much more efficient way because she was able to effectively communicate with her clients in a way that was best for them.

Playbook Exercise 22 - Favorable Introduction Script

(see p. 154)

Back again to our Master Coach Mark Sheer...

Most of us have experienced the power of an introduction from an "A" client or Center of Influence (COI). When you first contact their referrals, the trust and goodwill of their relationship with your referral source will transfer to you. This will open a brief window of opportunity, allowing you to immediately begin to bond with their referrals and embark on your own secure relationship as their trusted Advisor.

Your Ideal Client Profile is a powerful tool. It defines your ideal client—those to whom you can provide the most help. It helps your referral source identify and introduce you to qualified referrals and professionals with whom you can develop lasting, mutually beneficial partnerships. In addition, it defines the problems you can resolve and how you can help your partners reach their vision of their ideal future. You will receive many more qualified referrals and powerful Introductions if you and your referral sources have a clear, specific picture of *who* and *how* you can help.

Once you have shared your Ideal Client Profile and you receive referrals by leveraging the referring clients lists, i.e., cell phone, linked-in or Facebook and you receive three or more qualified client names, simply ask your client or Center of Influence: "What would be the best way for you to introduce me to these folks so they will want to meet with me and I can help them like I've helped you and your family (or business)?"

Remember you can get introduced in-person, 3-way conference call, email, voice mail or even a letter (if necessary).

We suggest your introductions follow this simple pattern: "Hey Bob, as you know I do not usually make introductions to other professionals, but I wanted to introduce you to my trusted Advisor and friend (Advisor first and last name and company name). (Advisor's first name) has helped me with (what you have done for the referring party) and I believe you could benefit from (what the referring party suggests).

"I have asked (Advisors first name) to call you. Please take her/his call so he/she can get to know a little about you and your goals for your future, and quantify the value that she/he can bring to you bring to you (and your family or business). I'm certain you'll be glad you spoke with her/him.

"Please keep me posted and let me know how things progress and best of success with your financial planning."

Bottom line, when our best students master the Get More "A" Clients favorable-introduction process tell us they convert between 60% and 90% of the favorable introductions they receive.

Chapter Seven

Accountability, Action and Achievement

Objectives	Action Item(s)
Goal for Week 7: Pull it all together and decide how to leverage on-going coaching to refine the process, implement to success and perpetuate success for exponential growth. **Key Topics:** ☐ Review and refine the Favorable Introduction strategy ☐ Review and refine the PAC 'MAP' (Q&A) ☐ Introduce "Perpetual Success Conditioning" and Next Steps	**Action (for review on week 7):** ☐ Complete "Coaching Maximizer" ☐ Commit to using the Client Review Agenda and Script on all ideal client annual reviews ☐ Commit to on-going coaching for implementation, accountability and perpetual success

PAC "Peak Performance through Self-Awareness - MAP for Accelerated Success": Week 7

Objectives: This is a 'wrap up' and 'transition' week where we bring our work so far to a close with a debrief on what we've covered, successes, opportunities for improvement and some options for continued accountability and refinement through coaching.

Specifically, you will walk away with:

- A complete action/business plan for the next 12 months with refinements.

- A clear understanding of how to use the "favorable introduction" strategy going forward to refine your book of business into more desirable clients that are fun and profitable to work with.

- Shared successes and takeaways.

- Specific options to sustain or build upon the momentum created through the "Off-Season" so far.

Way to GO!

Now what?

We encourage you to continue referring back to this Off-Season Playbook while reviewing your MAP - Momentum Action Plan on a regular basis. Your MAP should serve as a living, breathing MAP for your business and future success. We look forward to hearing about all your successes in the days, weeks and years to come.

On a final closing note, in order to track progress, measure change and provide a return on your investment, the Off-Season Playbook coach track utilizes four different tracking reviews:

1. MAP - Momentum Action Plan (reviewed quarterly)

2. KPIs (Key Performance Indicators) (reviewed weekly)

3. Strategies (reviewed daily)

4. Projects and Daily Metrics (reviewed weekly)

God Bless!
Sincerely,
Walter Bond and Rich Campe

Action Items – Exercise Check List

Awareness... It All Starts With You!

Exercises from Chapter One

Playbook Exercise 1 - The MindScan (see p. 6)

MindScan

The MindScan system will help you understand your natural thinking strengths by looking at two divisions, your *internal world* and your *external world*. Your external world is the world in which you react and interact with other people and situations. Your internal world relates to your personal thoughts and perceptions about yourself.

To better understand these two worlds, we break each into three separate dimensions.

- To create order and structure we all have a way to define "The Way It Should Be."

- On a daily basis we have a need to solve problems and choose options, "The Way It Could Be."

- Finally, we have a way in which we view others and ourselves, "Who I Am."

There is not a thought that any of us has or an action that we take that is not based upon one of these three dimensions. Let's take a look at the impact of each of these dimensions in our life:

Understanding Your Internal and External World

The Way It Should Be: In our external world, this measures our need for a defined environment, an environment based upon a perception of the way things should be done. It includes our perceptions of the need for rules, guidelines, rights and wrongs. In our internal world, it measures our sense of direction, the degree to which we have a firm set of guidelines and plans as to what we should and should not do. It is the need for structure we apply to our lives in both worlds.

The Way It Could Be: Given this need for structure or lack of it, this measures, in our external world, our ability to consider a wide range of options in achieving a solution or maximizing an opportunity. The greater our thinking strength in this dimension, the more options we're able to consider. In our lives, we all choose a wide range of roles—husband, mother, parent, etc. In your internal world, this Dimension measures our ability to make these choices and our level of satisfaction as we seek our own personal solutions and opportunities.

Who am I: Once we decide what should be accomplished (Should Be) and we've determined what could be accomplished (Could Be), this third dimension measures our ability to read and relate to others and ourselves as we actively pursue our objectives. As an external world measurement, it has nothing to do with personality. Internally, it is a measure of our self-esteem, our ability to understand and relate to ourselves, to see ourselves as unique. It is an indicator of our ability to feel good about our accomplishments and ourselves.

My Initial Thoughts

Before taking the MindScan, you will complete the following evaluation of yourself in five key areas. First, read the definition of the key area and then record your thoughts regarding your own life according to this category. This will provide a valuable tool in evaluating your own perceptions against the reality of your strengths and weaknesses.

Remember, there are only right answers.

Empathy

What is Empathy and Why is it Important?

It is fundamental: If we want to understand why people behave the way they do, we must begin by understanding how they feel. Feelings are the source of our motivations, our hopes, our fears, our distractions, and our drives. In addition, our feelings form the foundation for our sense of loyalty and commitment. Our individual feelings make us unique. Being aware of this uniqueness is as essential in management as it is in everyday life. Respect is appreciation for each person's uniqueness. To maximize effectiveness in dealing with people, we must treat them with respect. The overall measure of our sensitivity to the feelings of and respect for others is *empathy*; it is our ability to read and understand other persons.

How Empathetic am I?

Clarity—Circle the number that applies.

1   2   3   4   5   6   7   8   9   10

BLIND   EXCEPTIONAL

Bias—Circle the number that applies.

1   2   3   4   5   6   7   8   9   10

UNDERUTILIZED   OVER UTILIZED

Comments

_____

_____

_____

_____

_____

_____

_____

Practical Thinking

What is Practical Thinking and Why is it Important?

Practical thinking is seeing the relevant and important within the complex. On a daily basis, we face a host of complicated problems and issues, at home, at work, and in between. All of which demand our attention. Complex problems usually require a great deal of effort and concentration. We must analyze all the relevant parts of a problem to see how each part affects other parts and the whole. Only then can we come to a conclusion about which parts are primary and critical and which are secondary. Because it requires understanding how to accomplish tasks effectively, we could call practical thinking our capacity for production management. This becomes the dimension where we seek results.

What is the importance of Practical Thinking in my life?

Clarity—Circle the number that applies.

1   2   3   4   5   6   7   8   9   10

BLIND   EXCEPTIONAL

Bias—Circle the number that applies.

1 2 3 4 5 6 7 8 9 10

UNDERUTILIZED   OVER UTILIZED

Comments

_____

_____

_____

Structured Thinking

<u>What is Structured Thinking and Why is it Important?</u>

Structured thinking creates the rules, policies, standards, laws, organization, and plans that govern our lives. For the architect, structured thinking becomes the blue print. For the computer programmer, it is the functional specification and the computer software code. For the CEO, it is the mission statement, the business plan and the organizational chart. For the manager, it is the production plan, sales plan, etc. In society, it is the customs we live by and the laws we submit to. At home, it is the standards of behavior we use for our children and ourselves. Because it is the logic which guides all our various ways of being in the world, it utilizes our ability to abstract from specific details. This allows us to see patterns of development in the light of the overall perspective.

It gives us benchmarks to measure our progress. Often unfairly stereotyped and maligned, structured thinking is critical to organization and perspective. Without structured thinking, we can easily go astray.

What is the importance of Structured Thinking in my life?

Clarity—Circle the number that applies.

1   2   3   4   5   6   7   8   9   10

BLIND   EXCEPTIONAL

Bias—Circle the number that applies.

1   2   3   4   5   6   7   8   9   10

UNDERUTILIZED   OVER UTILIZED

Comments

_____

_____

_____

Self Esteem

What is Self Esteem and Why is it Important?

If we want to understand why we behave the way we do, we must begin by understanding the esteem in which we hold ourselves. *Self-esteem* is value we place on our own life. It is how we feel about ourselves, the estimation of our own worth. The feelings which generate our motivations and commitments also make us unique. Esteem is the measure of how we value our own uniqueness. That esteem should be genuine respect, a real appreciation of our own uniqueness. Persons with low self-esteem are hindered in marshaling their strengths and are blocked from acting effectively. High self-esteem, if properly governed, can be the source of creative and constructive action. The overall measure of our sensitivity to the feelings of and respect for one's self is self esteem; it is our ability to read, understand, and appreciate ourselves.

How would I describe my Self Esteem?

Clarity—Circle the number that applies.

1 2 3 4 5 6 7 8 9 10

BLIND   EXCEPTIONAL

Bias—Circle the number that applies.

1 2 3 4 5 6 7 8 9 10

UNDERUTILIZED   OVER UTILIZED

Comments

_____

_____

_____

Role Awareness

What is Role Awareness and Why is it Important?

Role awareness is understanding how you fit into your world. All of us play many different roles. We are employees, spouses, parents, managers, friends, neighbors and citizens. How we see ourselves functioning in these roles: our effectiveness, our importance and our desire to be an important role player is being measured in this score. Understanding and appreciating the importance of performing a given role requires the attention necessary for success. Furthermore, we must be convinced of our own importance and value in the role to be empowered to succeed.

What is the importance of Role Awareness in my life?

Clarity—Circle the number that applies.

1   2   3   4   5   6   7   8   9   10

BLIND   EXCEPTIONAL

Bias—Circle the number that applies.

1   2   3   4   5   6   7   8   9   10

UNDERUTILIZED   OVER UTILIZED

Comments

_____

_____

_____

Self-Direction

What is Self Direction and Why is it Important?

Self-direction is our understanding of our own values, ideals, commitments, and goals. Self-direction is the measure of the person we believe we are and want to be. It represents that which we strive to achieve and perfect - our very standards of integrity, honesty, diligence, and reliability. In a word, self-direction represents our character. Being clear about our own self-direction makes it possible for us to be consistent and reliable. Our sense of self-direction directly affects the manner in which other people interact with us. The standards by which we hold ourselves accountable reflect themselves in the expectations others have of us. The more clearly we project reliable standards to others, the more trust others will invest in us. Self-direction is a picture of the ethical person we intend to be. It forms the rational building blocks of our own projection of ourselves.

What is the importance of Self Direction in my life?

Clarity—Circle the number that applies.

1   2   3   4   5   6   7   8   9   10

BLIND   EXCEPTIONAL

Bias—Circle the number that applies.

1   2   3   4   5   6   7   8   9   10

UNDERUTILIZED   OVER UTILIZED

Comments

_____

_____

_____

Taking the MindScan Profile

With this basic understanding of the Internal and External Worlds, we now invite you to participate in our Online MindScan. The process will take about 20 minutes so make sure you have a block of uninterrupted time before beginning.

Directions:
1. Open a web browser and go to the website address www.ProAdvisorCoach.com/offseason
2. Enter your contact information
3. Take Part 1 and Part 2 of the MindScan

A ProAdvisor Coach will be notified of the completion of your MindScan and will contact you to review the results. To take the MindScan go to the following link : www.ProAdvisor Coach.com/offseason

Playbook Exercise 2 - Success Questionnaire (see p. 9)

Success Questionnaire

Knowing Who You Are...
You will learn more about yourself by answering these questions. There are only correct answers.

Where Am I?
This is an initial ranking of your Life Areas. Please complete this before beginning any other part of this course.

Rank the Following Life Areas 1—10
(1 being the worst and 10 being the best)

Physical Health and Vitality:

Nutrition	Worst 1 2 3 4 5 6 7 8 9 10 Best
Structure and Flexibility	Worst 1 2 3 4 5 6 7 8 9 10 Best
Physical Strength	Worst 1 2 3 4 5 6 7 8 9 10 Best
Aerobic and Endurance	Worst 1 2 3 4 5 6 7 8 9 10 Best

Relationships:

Family	Worst 1 2 3 4 5 6 7 8 9 10 Best
Work	Worst 1 2 3 4 5 6 7 8 9 10 Best
Friends	Worst 1 2 3 4 5 6 7 8 9 10 Best

Spiritual, Purpose and Destiny:

Connection · · · · · · · · · · Worst 1 2 3 4 5 6 7 8 9 10 Best

Certainty · · · · · · · · · · · Worst 1 2 3 4 5 6 7 8 9 10 Best

Growth · · · · · · · · · · · · · Worst 1 2 3 4 5 6 7 8 9 10 Best

Contribution · · · · · · · · · Worst 1 2 3 4 5 6 7 8 9 10 Best

Significance · · · · · · · · · Worst 1 2 3 4 5 6 7 8 9 10 Best

Variety · · · · · · · · · · · · · Worst 1 2 3 4 5 6 7 8 9 10 Best

Financial:

Short Term Cash Flow · · · Worst 1 2 3 4 5 6 7 8 9 10 Best

Mid Range Income · · · · · · Worst 1 2 3 4 5 6 7 8 9 10 Best

Long Term Income · · · · · · Worst 1 2 3 4 5 6 7 8 9 10 Best

1. How do you define "Success?"

2. Do you personally know anyone who lives what you consider "success?" If so, by what name or nick name may we refer to them by during our coaching?

- What do these associates have in their lives that tell you they are successful?

- What would you like to comment on regarding the characteristics or habits of these people?

3. Do you know of anyone (not personally) who lives what you consider "success?" If so, by what name or nick name may we refer to them by during our coaching?

- What do these people have in their lives that show you they are successful?

- What would you like to comment on regarding the characteristics or habits of these people?

4. What percentage of the time do you find yourself focused on problems and difficulties?

5. What percentage of the time do you view yourself as responsible for the results in your life (as opposed to a victim of accident)?

6. Are you consciously aware of the words you choose when talking to yourself?

7. If you were to ask a dear friend if your words are predominantly empowering or limiting, what would be the reply?

8. What book(s) have impacted your life? What did you get personally from it (them)?

9. What book(s) are you currently reading? What are you getting from them?

10. Of the above rewards from reading, what are or have you applied to your life?

11. What books are next on your "to read" list?

12. Who do the people you currently surround yourself with inspire you to be?

13. If you would change anything about your choice of people you choose to surround yourself with, what improvements would you make?

14. What interests you most about Professional Coaching?

15. How did you decide to commit to this Coaching Solution?

16. Describe any direct/indirect experience you've had with personal coaching:

17. What is your current occupation?

18. What occupational goals do you have?

19. Briefly, what is your occupational history?

20. What is (are) your greatest personal strength(s)?

21. If you could improve one thing in your life that would dramatically improve all aspects, what would it be?

22. What different leadership responsibilities do you have? (Career; Personal; Family; Community...etc)

23. What is your purpose in life?

24. What is your mission in life?

25. What does success look, feel or sound like to you?

26 Why did you invest your time in answering these questions?

Playbook Exercise 3 - Coaching Readiness (see p. 11)

Coach Readiness Index – Committing to the Next Level

Are you ready to commit taking your life and/or profession to the next level?!? Let's see. **Rate each statement from *least* true (1) to *most* true (5)**. Total your points and enter at the bottom, "Total Score." This score will provide you and your coach some insight on how well the coaching will work for you. Perhaps with some advance discussion, you may feel more prepared to score higher in some areas or at a minimum, enter into the relationship with eyes wide open.

		You can count on me to commit time to meet with my coach.
		The timing feels right for me to embrace coaching and I'm willing to be "real" (that means a willingness to be vulnerable and trust).
		I'm ready to commit to complete the work and I agree to be accountable for without struggling or sabotaging (procrastination and diversions) and allow my coach to coach me.
		I'll give my coach the benefit of the doubt and "try on" new concepts or different ways of doing things, even if it's uncomfortable or stretches me.
		I will speak truthfully and be real with my coach without fear of judgment from, hurting or offending him/her.
		If I feel that I am not getting what I need or expect from my coach, I will share this as soon as I sense it and express what I want and need from the relationship.

		I am willing to eliminate or modify the self-defeating behaviors which limit my success.
		I have adequate funds to pay for professional coaching and will not regret or suffer over the fees. I see coaching as a worthwhile and lifelong investment.
		I am someone who can share the credit for my success with my coach.
		I am either ready to take my life and profession to the next level or ready for a major breakout from where I am today.
		Total Score (add up all above scores)

Scoring Key

10-20 Probably **not** a good timing for coaching right now.

21-30 Reasonably Coachable; but make sure ground rules are honored!

31-40 Coachable; great time for coaching, a major breakthrough is within reach... take the next step!

41-50 Very coachable; a major breakthrough is within grasp so ask the coach to ask a lot from you!

Playbook Exercise 4 - Sweet Spot Analysis (see p. 14)

Sweet Spot Analysis

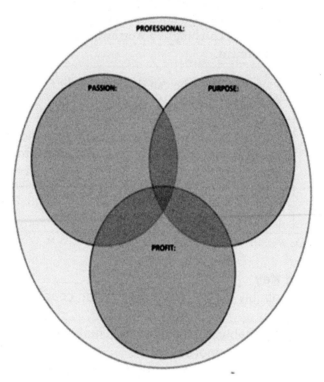

Purpose:

If time, money and energy were not obstacles, what could you become the very best at in this business? List the things that you are exceptionally good at performing. List the things people tell you that you are good at doing. List the things that naturally come easy to you.

_____

_____

_____

_____

_____

_____

_____

_____

_____

_____

_____

_____

_____

_____

_____

_____

Passion:

What are the actions, tasks and projects you enjoy most about your career and in life? What do you get excited about doing? What actions or projects do you tend to lose yourself in or lose track of time? When you are in the Zone , what is it that you are doing?

_____

_____

_____

_____

_____

_____

_____

_____

_____

_____

_____

_____

_____

_____

Profit:

From the Purpose and Passion lists notice what actions, tasks and projects were on both of those. Transfer those overlapping items to this list. Now rank them in order of highest revenue producing activities. The top three items on this list make up your Sweet Spot. You must find a way to spend as much of your professional time in your Sweet Spot. Anything else that lies outside of that sweet spot must be limited, eliminated, delegated or outsourced.

_____
_____
_____
_____
_____
_____
_____
_____
_____
_____
_____
_____
_____
_____

Professional:

In any profession, there are going to be tasks, projects and actions you may not feel are on purpose for you, nor do you have a passion for. However, they must be done by you to hold yourself out as a professional. This might include things like compliance, continuing education etc.

List those items here.

Playbook Exercise 5 - Core Disciplines (see p. 16)

Advisor Core Disciplines Score Card

The Core Disciplines in this scorecard are those that have been found to be fundamental determinants of success in marketing and selling financial and other professional services. At different stages of your career, some disciplines may have more relevance for you than others. As you review the effectiveness in each discipline, identify opportunities to further leverage those that are strengths and to shore up those that are weaknesses.

This exercise will be used in the PAC Affinity Plan coaching process to help you develop an executable plan with effective Key Performance Indicators (KPIs) and Strategies to achieve your vision for your business or career.

To complete this exercise, rate your effectiveness on a scale of 1-10 the 1 being not effective and 10 being very effective. Then, list the improvements that you need to make and/or have made by your firm or company.

1. Ideal Client Profile:

How well defined is your Client Profile? (Circle one)

1 2 3 4 5 6 7 8 9 10

Why did you give it this score?

_____

_____

_____

_____

_____

What improvements are needed?

_____

_____

_____

_____

_____

Are you seeing enough prospective clients who would fall into this Ideal Client Profile? (Circle one)

1   2   3   4   5   6   7   8   9   10

Why did you give it this score?

_____

_____

_____

_____

_____

What improvements are needed?

_____

_____

_____

_____

2. Target Market:

How effective are you at focusing on your target market(s)?

1   2   3   4   5   6   7   8   9   10

Why did you give it this score?

_____

_____

_____

_____

_____

What improvements are needed?

_____

_____

_____

_____

_____

3. Unique Value Offer:

How effective and compelling are your products, services and 'add value offerings?"

1   2   3   4   5   6   7   8   9   10

Why did you give it this score?

_____

_____

_____

_____

_____

What Improvements are needed?

_____

_____

_____

_____

_____

4. "Referral" Process:

How effective is your referral process at consistently producing quality leads? [Referral sources can include any or all of past clients, current clients, your business and community network of contacts, competitors, service providers, other professionals, etc.]

1   2   3   4   5   6   7   8   9   10

Why did you give it this score?

_____

_____

_____

_____

What improvements are needed?

_____

_____

_____

_____

5. Marketing and Sales Process:

Rate your marketing and sales process. How effective are you and your process at creating value and building trust for clients and potential clients?

1   2   3   4   5   6   7   8   9   10

Why did you give it this score?

_____

_____

_____

_____

_____

What improvements are needed?

_____

_____

_____

_____

_____

6. Technology:

How effective is your / your firm's / your company's client management system at building and maintaining the your client relationships and adding value for your clients?

1   2   3   4   5   6   7   8   9   10

Why did you give it this score?

_____
_____
_____
_____
_____

What improvements are needed?

_____
_____
_____
_____
_____

7. Personal Growth and Development:

Are you being intentional about scheduling time on a consistent basis to increase your Skills & Knowledge and maintain at least the minimum annual professional development hours required to maintain your professional designation(s) ?

1   2   3   4   5   6   7   8   9   10

Why did you give it this score?

_____

_____

_____

_____

_____

What improvements are needed?

_____

_____

_____

_____

_____

8. Strategic Execution:

How effectively do you and your people execute strategic priorities?

1   2   3   4   5   6   7   8   9   10

Why did you give it this score?

_____

_____

_____

_____

_____

What improvements are needed?

_____

_____

_____

_____

_____

9. Progress Measuring Process:

How well do you and your people use lead and lag indicators to make timely business decisions?

1   2   3   4   5   6   7   8   9   10

Why did you give it this score?

_____

_____

_____

_____

_____

What improvements are needed?

_____

_____

_____

_____

_____

10. Value Creation:

How effective are you at providing value for your direct reports, if applicable?

1   2   3   4   5   6   7   8   9   10

Why did you give it this score?

_____

_____

_____

_____

_____

What improvements are needed?

_____

_____

_____

_____

_____

11. Recruiting Process:

Rate your recruiting process for new professional and administrative staff, if this is part of your role in your firm/company. How effective are you at generating strong referrals and a consistent flow of quality candidates?

1   2   3   4   5   6   7   8   9   10

Why did you give it this score?

_____

_____

_____

_____

_____

What improvements are needed?

_____

_____

_____

_____

_____

12. Performance Coaching:

How effective are you at identifying, acting on, and coaching the members of your team (professional and administrative as applicable), including coaching on performance improvements and breakdowns on your team?

1   2   3   4   5   6   7   8   9   10

Why did you give it this score?

_____

_____

_____

_____

_____

What improvements are needed?

_____

_____

_____

_____

_____

13. Direct Report Development:

Do you have unique development plans for each Direct Report, if applicable?

1   2   3   4   5   6   7   8   9   10

Why did you give it this score?

_____

_____

_____

_____

_____

What improvements are needed?

_____

_____

_____

_____

_____

14. Communication:

How frequently and how well do you communicate your/ your firm's, your company's strategic and operational directions to your staff, if applicable?

1   2   3   4   5   6   7   8   9   10

Why did you give it this score?

_____

_____

_____

_____

_____

What improvements are needed?

_____
_____
_____
_____
_____

How well do you use communication to build and improve your team?

1   2   3   4   5   6   7   8   9   10

Why did you give it this score?

_____
_____
_____
_____
_____

What improvements are needed?

_____
_____
_____
_____
_____

Exercises From Chapter Two

Playbook Exercise 6 - Coaching Maximizer (see p. 21)

The Coaching Call/Meeting Maximizer

Complete and submit this form 24 - 48 hours prior to your coaching session with your achievement coach to gain maximum benefit from the coaching time!

My Name: _____

Today's Date: _____

Rank the Following Life Areas 1—10
(1 being the worst and 10 being the best)

Physical Health and Vitality:

Nutrition   Worst 1 2 3 4 5 6 7 8 9 10 Best

Structure and Flexibility   Worst 1 2 3 4 5 6 7 8 9 10 Best

Physical Strength   Worst 1 2 3 4 5 6 7 8 9 10 Best

Aerobic and Endurance   Worst 1 2 3 4 5 6 7 8 9 10 Best

Relationships:

Family   Worst 1 2 3 4 5 6 7 8 9 10 Best

Work   Worst 1 2 3 4 5 6 7 8 9 10 Best

Friends   Worst 1 2 3 4 5 6 7 8 9 10 Best

Spiritual, Purpose and Destiny:

Connection   Worst 1 2 3 4 5 6 7 8 9 10 Best

Certainty   Worst 1 2 3 4 5 6 7 8 9 10 Best

Growth   Worst 1 2 3 4 5 6 7 8 9 10 Best

Contribution   Worst 1 2 3 4 5 6 7 8 9 10 Best

Significance   Worst 1 2 3 4 5 6 7 8 9 10 Best

Variety   Worst 1 2 3 4 5 6 7 8 9 10 Best

Financial:

Short Term Cash Flow   Worst 1 2 3 4 5 6 7 8 9 10 Best

Mid Range Income   Worst 1 2 3 4 5 6 7 8 9 10 Best

Long Term Income   Worst 1 2 3 4 5 6 7 8 9 10 Best

Exercises From Chapter Two

1. What have I accomplished since our last session?

2. What are some of my wins?

3. Were there any commitments that I made, yet didn't complete? If so, what were they and why?

4. Do I have any BIG distractions or challenges right now? If so, what?

5. Do I have any significant opportunities available to me right now? If so, what?

6. This week, I made _____ entries into my Personal Journal.

7. As a result of working with my coach:

• What do I have that is different as a result of my last coaching session (RESULTS)?

- What am I doing that is different as a result of my last coaching session (ACTION)?

- Who am I being that is different as a result of my last coaching session (CHARACTER)?

8. Today, I am grateful for:

Important! Confirming my next coaching appointment

Date: _____ Time: _____ & Time Zone: _____

Comments:

_____

Playbook Exercise 7 -
MindScan on 3 significant relationships (see p. 22)

List below your key relationships in the following areas:

- Support Staff

- Business partners

- Strategic alliances

- Centers of influence

- Ideal clients

- Spouse or significant other

_____

_____

_____

_____

_____

_____

_____

_____

_____

_____

_____

_____

_____

Select three of these people to take the MindScan. Base these selections on the influence they have regarding the increase of your time, money and fun.

Go to the following website to access the MindScan for your significant relationships www.ProAdvisorCoach.com/offseason

You can send the link to the three people on your list to take the MindScan.

Playbook Exercise 8 - Ideal Client Profile (see p. 23)

Ideal Client Profile Exercise

*"**Star Customers** receive high value from a firm's products and services and provide high value in the form of high margins, loyalty, and retention. Companies should identify and build on this type of customer."*

"Customers are the lifeblood of any organization and the heart of the demand-driven economy. Scores of books have been written about the importance of customers, ways to provide value to them and the need for a company to be customer-oriented. Senior executives in all industries readily agree that customers are critical to the survival of a firm, that customers are their most valuable asset and that their entire organization must be customer-centric.

Businesses often make one of two big mistakes when it comes to customers: They either pay too little attention and risk losing them, or they work too hard at trying to keep the wrong ones. The key is learning about the customers that matter the most to your business and making sure they are happy.

Sunil Gupta and Bernard Schmitt, both professors and authors, write, "Rather than spread itself too thin by treating all customers the same, a company should identify its different types of customers and treat each group appropriately." Since Gupta and Schmitt's goal is to help a business create a customer-centric organization, some of their advice — like "firing" some customers who are too costly to maintain — is startling. "This may sound counterintuitive — be customer-focused, but don't invest in some customers," they write. "But a study of U.S. banks in the early '90s found that only 30% of customers were profitable over the long run — 70% of customers destroyed value!"

by Susan Cartier Liebel
(Instructor at "Solo Practice University")

This exercise is intended to help you create an "ideal client profile" that allows you to target prospects with greater efficiency and accuracy. The benefits are clear:

- Attract more qualified prospects

- Improve conversion rates

- Create raving fans and retain clients longer

- Increase additional business from existing clients

- Enjoy your work more with clients that are a better fit

Directions: Think about your top 5-10 VERY BEST clients. Answer the following questions describing your "ideal client" to the best of your ability. Keep in mind, this is a "magic wand" exercise where the question is...if you could build your business with only "ideal clients", what attributes would most of them have in common?

Demographics...

Age range?

Gender focus?

Religious preferences?

Geography where they live or work?

With or without children?

Profession or industry in which they work?

Role or title?

Other (ex. – net worth, investable assets, annual income, etc.)?

Psychographics...

What attributes do they posses? (Passion, consistency, committed)

_____

_____

What are they passionate about?

_____

_____

What types of people do they spend time with?

_____

_____

What do they value most?

_____

_____

Where do they spend most of their time?

_____

_____

What do they do in their spare time?

_____

_____

How do they learn and where do they like to go to learn?

_____

_____

What do they read? When do they read it? Where do they read?

_____

_____

What shops, Web sites, etc. do they purchase products from or visit most?

_____

_____

What social media resources do they use most?

_____

_____

What organizations, meetings, groups, and classes do they attend?

_____

_____

What type of people are you attracting to your business?

_____

_____

What are the critical wants, needs and expectations these Ideal Clients have you aim to satisfy?

_____

_____

What do they want more of?

_____

_____

What do they want less of?

_____

_____

What do they expect?

_____

_____

What else??

_____

_____

Creating VSI and UVP (Value Specific Identity & Unique Value Proposition)...

How are you uniquely gifted, passionate and/or resourced to satisfy their needs better than most?

_____

_____

What experience do you have that would help you satisfy their needs better than most?

_____

_____

What resources do you have that would help you satisfy their needs better than most?

_____

_____

How do you want to be seen by these clients...what do you want them to say about you?

_____

_____

How are you uniquely positioned to find and connect with your ideal clients?

_____

_____

Lead Generation Strategies...

- Ideal clients
- Ideal alliance partners
- Ideal centers of influence
- Seminars & workshops
- Other??

The MAP "Momentum Action Plan" – Part I

Exercises From Chapter Three

Playbook Exercise 9 - Coaching Maximizer (see p. 27)

The Coaching Call/Meeting Maximizer

Complete and submit this form 24 - 48 hours prior to your coaching session with your achievement coach to gain maximum benefit from the coaching time!

My Name: _____

Today's Date: _____

Rank the Following Life Areas 1—10
(1 being the worst and 10 being the best)

Physical Health and Vitality:

Nutrition   Worst 1 2 3 4 5 6 7 8 9 10 Best

Structure and Flexibility   Worst 1 2 3 4 5 6 7 8 9 10 Best

Physical Strength	Worst 1 2 3 4 5 6 7 8 9 10 Best
Aerobic and Endurance	Worst 1 2 3 4 5 6 7 8 9 10 Best

Relationships:

Family	Worst 1 2 3 4 5 6 7 8 9 10 Best
Work	Worst 1 2 3 4 5 6 7 8 9 10 Best
Friends	Worst 1 2 3 4 5 6 7 8 9 10 Best

Spiritual, Purpose and Destiny:

Connection	Worst 1 2 3 4 5 6 7 8 9 10 Best
Certainty	Worst 1 2 3 4 5 6 7 8 9 10 Best
Growth	Worst 1 2 3 4 5 6 7 8 9 10 Best
Contribution	Worst 1 2 3 4 5 6 7 8 9 10 Best
Significance	Worst 1 2 3 4 5 6 7 8 9 10 Best
Variety	Worst 1 2 3 4 5 6 7 8 9 10 Best

Financial:

Short Term Cash Flow	Worst 1 2 3 4 5 6 7 8 9 10 Best
Mid Range Income	Worst 1 2 3 4 5 6 7 8 9 10 Best
Long Term Income	Worst 1 2 3 4 5 6 7 8 9 10 Best

Exercises From Chapter Three

1. What have I accomplished since our last session?

2. What are some of my wins?

3. Were there any commitments that I made, yet didn't complete? If so, what were they and why?

4. Do I have any BIG distractions or challenges right now? If so, what?

5. Do I have any significant opportunities available to me right now? If so, what?

6. This week, I made _____ entries into my Personal Journal.

7. As a result of working with my coach:

- What do I have that is different as a result of my last coaching session (RESULTS)?

- What am I doing that is different as a result of my last coaching session (ACTION)?

- Who am I being that is different as a result of my last coaching session (CHARACTER)?

8. Today, I am grateful for:

Important! Confirming my next coaching appointment

Date: _____ Time: _____ & Time Zone: _____

Comments:

_____
_____
_____
_____
_____
_____
_____
_____
_____
_____
_____

Playbook Exercise 10, 11 and 12 -
Vision, Mission and Values (see p. 27 and 31)

VISION STATEMENT

Passion Drives Vision

If you already have a dream or vision for your life, what is it? Otherwise skip.

_____

_____

_____

_____

List three things you're extremely passionate about?

1. _____

2. _____

3. _____

3. If you could be assured of success in any venture, what major accomplishments would you achieve in your lifetime?

_____

_____

_____

4. If you acknowledge and are in touch with a higher power, where do you sense it leading your life?

_____

_____

_____

5. How do you see yourself & your profession in 10, 20 or 30 years?

10 years

_____
_____
_____
_____
_____
_____
_____

20 years

_____
_____
_____
_____
_____
_____

30 years

_____
_____
_____
_____
_____
_____

Personal Values & Priorities

1. Of the following values or virtues, what are your **top 10**?

• Caring	• Compassionate	• Confident
• Considerate	• Consistent	• Contented
• Cooperative	• Courageous	• Creative
• Dedicated	• Dependable	• Diligent
• Enthusiastic	• Fair	• Flexible
• Forgiving	• Friendly	• Generous
• Gentle	• Giving	• Helpful
• Honest	• Humble	• Joyful
• Kind	• Loving	• Loyal
• Merciful	• Obedient	• Patient
• Peaceful	• Reliable	• Respectful
• Responsible	• Self-controlled	• Self-disciplined
• Sensitive	• Sincere	• Supportive
• Teachable	• Thankful	• Tolerant
• Trusting	• Trustworthy	• Unselfish

2. List 5-10 things that you hope to obtain during your life?

1. _____

2. _____

3. _____

4. _____

5. _____

6. _____

7. _____

8. _____

9. _____

10. _____

Mission, Purpose & Legacy

Who are the 5-10 individuals or groups that you hope to help during the course of your life?

1. _____

2. _____

3. _____

4. _____

5. _____

6. _____

7. _____

8. _____

9. _____

10. _____

What are the 5-10 major accomplishments that you hope to have achieved during your life?

1. _____

2. _____

3. _____

4. _____

5. _____

6. _____

7. _____

8. _____

9. _____

10. _____

Based on your life experience, what makes you feel complete and whole?

_____
_____
_____
_____
_____

Based on your life experience, what are you really good at?

_____
_____
_____
_____
_____

What positive personal feedback have other important people in your life given you (things they've commended you on, raved about, observed about you, etc.)?

_____
_____
_____
_____
_____

At the end of your life, what legacy would you want to leave the world?

_____

_____

_____

_____

_____

What would you most like the people at your funeral to say about you specifically?

_____

_____

_____

_____

_____

Complete this sentence: As I take my final breaths on this earth and look back on my life, I will have minimal (or no) regrets if I...

_____

_____

_____

_____

_____

Who in history do you admire most, and what does that say about me?

_____

_____

_____

_____

_____

If you could solve a world problem, what would it be? Be very specific please.

_____

_____

_____

_____

_____

If you knew what your life purpose or mission was, what does your gut tell you it would be?

_____

_____

_____

_____

_____

Personal Vision & Mission Statement:
(Reflect back on your prior answers.)

1. These are the main things that motivate me/bring me joy and satisfaction:

2. My greatest strengths/abilities/traits/things I do best:

3. At least two things I can start doing/do more often that use my strengths and bring me joy:

4. Personal **Vision Statement** (how do you envision yourself ~ < 50 words):

5. My Personal **Mission/Purpose Statement** (in 50 words or less):

The MAP "Momentum Action Plan" – Part II

Exercises From Chapter Four

Playbook Exercise 13 - Coaching Maximizer (see p. 35)

The Coaching Call/Meeting Maximizer

Complete and submit this form 24 - 48 hours prior to your coaching session with your achievement coach to gain maximum benefit from the coaching time!

My Name: _____

Today's Date: _____

Rank the Following Life Areas 1—10
(1 being the worst and 10 being the best)

Physical Health and Vitality:

Nutrition   Worst 1 2 3 4 5 6 7 8 9 10 Best

Structure and Flexibility   Worst 1 2 3 4 5 6 7 8 9 10 Best

Physical Strength	Worst 1 2 3 4 5 6 7 8 9 10 Best
Aerobic and Endurance	Worst 1 2 3 4 5 6 7 8 9 10 Best

Relationships:

Family	Worst 1 2 3 4 5 6 7 8 9 10 Best
Work	Worst 1 2 3 4 5 6 7 8 9 10 Best
Friends	Worst 1 2 3 4 5 6 7 8 9 10 Best

Spiritual, Purpose and Destiny:

Connection	Worst 1 2 3 4 5 6 7 8 9 10 Best
Certainty	Worst 1 2 3 4 5 6 7 8 9 10 Best
Growth	Worst 1 2 3 4 5 6 7 8 9 10 Best
Contribution	Worst 1 2 3 4 5 6 7 8 9 10 Best
Significance	Worst 1 2 3 4 5 6 7 8 9 10 Best
Variety	Worst 1 2 3 4 5 6 7 8 9 10 Best

Financial:

Short Term Cash Flow	Worst 1 2 3 4 5 6 7 8 9 10 Best
Mid Range Income	Worst 1 2 3 4 5 6 7 8 9 10 Best
Long Term Income	Worst 1 2 3 4 5 6 7 8 9 10 Best

Exercises From Chapter Four

1. What have I accomplished since our last session?

2. What are some of my wins?

3. Were there any commitments that I made, yet didn't complete? If so, what were they and why?

4. Do I have any BIG distractions or challenges right now? If so, what?

5. Do I have any significant opportunities available to me right now? If so, what?

6. This week, I made _____ entries into my Personal Journal.

7. As a result of working with my coach:

- What do I have that is different as a result of my last coaching session (RESULTS)?

- What am I doing that is different as a result of my last coaching session (ACTION)?

- Who am I being that is different as a result of my last coaching session (CHARACTER)?

8. Today, I am grateful for:

Important! Confirming my next coaching appointment

Date: _____ Time: _____ & Time Zone: _____

Comments:

_____
_____
_____
_____
_____
_____
_____
_____
_____
_____
_____

Playbook Exercise 14 - Activity Planner (see p. 35

Create Your MAP - Momentum Action Plan

Company Name: _____

Fiscal Year: _____

Vision:

_____
_____
_____
_____
_____

Mission:

_____
_____
_____
_____
_____

Values:

_____
_____
_____
_____
_____

The Off-Season for Financial Advisors

Focus Areas:

_____

_____

_____

_____

_____

KPI's - Key Performance Indicators:

_____

_____

_____

_____

_____

Strategies:

_____

_____

_____

_____

_____

Projects:

_____

_____

_____

_____

_____

Critical Activities:

_____

_____

_____

_____

_____

Playbook Exercise 15 - Ideal Clients (see p. 38)

List your Qualified, Committed and Coachable Ideal Clients below. This should be about 10% - 20% of your entire client base.

1. _____
2. _____
3. _____
4. _____
5. _____
6. _____
7. _____
8. _____
9. _____
10. _____
11. _____
12. _____
13. _____
14. _____
15. _____
16. _____
17. _____
18. _____
19. _____
20. _____
21. _____
22. _____
23. _____
24. _____

25. _____
26. _____
27. _____
28. _____
29. _____
30. _____
31. _____
32. _____
33. _____
34. _____
35. _____
36. _____
37. _____
38. _____
39. _____
40. _____

Playbook Exercise 16 - Sales Funnel (see p. 40)

List your current sales funnel by week

Week: _____

Appointments Scheduled: _____

Appointments Kept: _____

Cases Opened: _____

Cases Closed: _____

Revenue Closed: _____ $ _____

Qualified, Committed and Coachable Relationships scheduled: ____

New Favorable Introductions from QCC's: _____

Exercises From Chapter Five

Playbook Exercise 17 - Coaching Maximizer (see p. 44)

The Coaching Call/Meeting Maximizer

Complete and submit this form 24 - 48 hours prior to your coaching session with your achievement coach to gain maximum benefit from the coaching session!

My Name: _____

Today's Date: _____

Rank the Following Life Areas 1—10
(1 being the worst and 10 being the best)

Physical Health and Vitality:

Nutrition   Worst 1 2 3 4 5 6 7 8 9 10 Best

Structure and Flexibility   Worst 1 2 3 4 5 6 7 8 9 10 Best

Physical Strength   Worst 1 2 3 4 5 6 7 8 9 10 Best

Aerobic and Endurance   Worst 1 2 3 4 5 6 7 8 9 10 Best

Relationships:

Family   Worst 1 2 3 4 5 6 7 8 9 10 Best

Work   Worst 1 2 3 4 5 6 7 8 9 10 Best

Friends   Worst 1 2 3 4 5 6 7 8 9 10 Best

Spiritual, Purpose and Destiny:

Connection   Worst 1 2 3 4 5 6 7 8 9 10 Best

Certainty   Worst 1 2 3 4 5 6 7 8 9 10 Best

Growth   Worst 1 2 3 4 5 6 7 8 9 10 Best

Contribution   Worst 1 2 3 4 5 6 7 8 9 10 Best

Significance   Worst 1 2 3 4 5 6 7 8 9 10 Best

Variety   Worst 1 2 3 4 5 6 7 8 9 10 Best

Financial:

Short Term Cash Flow   Worst 1 2 3 4 5 6 7 8 9 10 Best

Mid Range Income   Worst 1 2 3 4 5 6 7 8 9 10 Best

Long Term Income   Worst 1 2 3 4 5 6 7 8 9 10 Best

Exercises From Chapter Five

1. What have I accomplished since our last session?

2. What are some of my wins?

3. Were there any commitments that I made, yet didn't complete? If so, what were they and why?

4. Do I have any BIG distractions or challenges right now? If so, what?

5. Do I have any significant opportunities available to me right now? If so, what?

6. This week, I made _____ entries into my Personal Journal.

7. As a result of working with my coach:

• What do I have that is different as a result of my last coaching session (RESULTS)?

- What am I doing that is different as a result of my last coaching session (ACTION)?

- Who am I being that is different as a result of my last coaching session (CHARACTER)?

8. Today, I am grateful for:

Important! Confirming my next coaching appointment

Date: _____ Time: _____ & Time Zone: _____

Comments:

_____
_____
_____
_____
_____
_____
_____
_____
_____
_____
_____

Playbook Exercise 18 - Ideal Week (see p. 45)

Ideal Week Tracker

1 Week Time Tracker

> *We are what we repeatedly do.*
> *Excellence, then, is not an act, but a habit.*
>
> *- Aristotle*

This exercise has three purposes:

1. Create awareness in how you actually spend your time.

2. Identify your "optimal zone."

3. Develop knowledge and skills to move more intentionally into your "zone" and towards your vision.

Have you ever looked back on your day and said, "WOW, it was a busy day today", yet still feel like you didn't get much done? Why is that?

Stephen Covey, best-selling author and speaker, suggests that every activity can be put into one of four quadrants:

	Urgent	**Not Urgent**
Important	QUADRANT I crises, pressing problems, deadline-driven projects ~ working in your life and business	QUADRANT II prevention, PC activities, relationship building, recognizing new opportunities, planning, recreation ~ working on your life and business

Not important	QUADRANT III interruptions, some calls, some mail, some reports, some meetings, popular activities ~ working in your life and business	QUADRANT IV trivia, busy work, some mail, some phone calls time wasters, pleasant activities

So, which quadrant are you spending the bulk of your time? This exercise will help you find out.

Once you know what you're doing with your time, we need to find out if that activity falls into your "optimal zone." What do we mean by that?

Your "optimal zone" is where your passion, strengths and critical success areas converge. This is where we need to spend most of our time which means designing your life and business in a way that allows this to happen more naturally through specialization and synergy. So with each activity you're involved with, ask yourself...

- How much do I enjoy or am I passionate about this?

- How much does this leverage my most valuable strengths?

- How much does this align with my "Big Game" and "Vision?"

Once we clearly see what we're doing and decide if the activity is within our "optimal zone", we then have to decide what to do! This is where the rubber meets the road and boils down to one questions... Should I do it now, defer it, delegate it or just say "NO" to it?

Although this may be slightly outside the scope of this exercise, here are some quick tips for managing your time a little better.

When to Say "No"

To be effective, you need to stay out of Quadrants III and IV. To do this, you need to tell yourself and other people "no" when it comes to activities in these areas. You won't likely experience the utopia of living 100% in Quadrant II, but moving in that direction should be your goal.

Weekly Organizing

Plan your week instead of your day. Each Sunday, look at your Scorecard and decide what, if any, changes need to be made. Where you fell short, decide what activities you prioritized over your core and baseline activities. Were they Quadrant I, III and IV activities? What do you need to do differently this week? What can you do to double and triple activities up, so that you're operating more efficiently? For example, go bike riding with your wife and son to combine family time and exercise.

Delegation & Specialization

Activities that must be done and lie outside our "optimal zone" are candidates for delegation. Your maximum potential will never be realized without interdependence. Yes, I said interdependence, not independence which tends to be the prevailing message in our culture. The power of leverage is clear when it comes to money but it also applies to others. By surrounding yourself with people who compliment your weaknesses or "optimal zone" and delegating to them the work that they do well and probably enjoy, your weaknesses become strengths and your strengths are used more often and powerfully.

The key to delegation is making sure what your delegating aligns with the other person's skills, knowledge and desire. From there, it's important to set clear expectations, empower them to get it done however they can do it best, provide adequate resources, establish check points and offer encouragement. Setting it up right makes it much easier to hold them accountable on the other end.

Now, start tracking your time and see how much of it you're spending in your "optimal zone." Have fun!

Instructions: For each 30 minute increment of time, briefly describe the activity in which you were engaged. To the right of it, rank how aligned it was with your "Big Game" from least to most, how well it leveraged your personal strengths from least to most and how much you enjoyed it from least to most. If you desire to do this over the weekend or beyond the times outlined, feel free to do so. Remember, there's no judgment here, just self awareness and improvement, so BE HONEST WITH YOURSELF and your coach!

	Monday	Big Game Rating 1=least 5=most	Strength Rating 1=least 5=most	Enjoyment Ranking 1=least 5=Most
7:00 AM				
7:30 AM				
8:00 AM				
8:30 AM				
9:00 AM				
9:30 AM				
10:00 AM				
10:30 AM				
11:00 AM				
11:30 AM				
12:00 PM				
12:30 PM				
1:00 PM				
1:30 PM				
2:00 PM				
2:30 PM				
3:00 PM				
3:30 PM				
4:00 PM				
4:30 PM				
5:00 PM				
5:30 PM				
6:00 PM				
6:30 PM				
7:00 PM				

The Off-Season for Financial Advisors

	Tuesday	Big Game Rating 1=least 5=most	Strength Rating 1=least 5=most	Enjoyment Ranking 1=least 5=Most
7:00 AM				
7:30 AM				
8:00 AM				
8:30 AM				
9:00 AM				
9:30 AM				
10:00 AM				
10:30 AM				
11:00 AM				
11:30 AM				
12:00 PM				
12:30 PM				
1:00 PM				
1:30 PM				
2:00 PM				
2:30 PM				
3:00 PM				
3:30 PM				
4:00 PM				
4:30 PM				
5:00 PM				
5:30 PM				
6:00 PM				
6:30 PM				
7:00 PM				

Exercises From Chapter Five

	Wednesday	Big Game Rating 1=least 5=most	Strength Rating 1=least 5=most	Enjoyment Ranking 1=least 5=Most
7:00 AM				
7:30 AM				
8:00 AM				
8:30 AM				
9:00 AM				
9:30 AM				
10:00 AM				
10:30 AM				
11:00 AM				
11:30 AM				
12:00 PM				
12:30 PM				
1:00 PM				
1:30 PM				
2:00 PM				
2:30 PM				
3:00 PM				
3:30 PM				
4:00 PM				
4:30 PM				
5:00 PM				
5:30 PM				
6:00 PM				
6:30 PM				
7:00 PM				

The Off-Season for Financial Advisors

	Thursday	Big Game Rating 1=least 5=most	Strength Rating 1=least 5=most	Enjoyment Ranking 1=least 5=Most
7:00 AM				
7:30 AM				
8:00 AM				
8:30 AM				
9:00 AM				
9:30 AM				
10:00 AM				
10:30 AM				
11:00 AM				
11:30 AM				
12:00 PM				
12:30 PM				
1:00 PM				
1:30 PM				
2:00 PM				
2:30 PM				
3:00 PM				
3:30 PM				
4:00 PM				
4:30 PM				
5:00 PM				
5:30 PM				
6:00 PM				
6:30 PM				
7:00 PM				

Exercises From Chapter Five

	Friday	Big Game Rating 1=least 5=most	Strength Rating 1=least 5=most	Enjoyment Ranking 1=least 5=Most
7:00 AM				
7:30 AM				
8:00 AM				
8:30 AM				
9:00 AM				
9:30 AM				
10:00 AM				
10:30 AM				
11:00 AM				
11:30 AM				
12:00 PM				
12:30 PM				
1:00 PM				
1:30 PM				
2:00 PM				
2:30 PM				
3:00 PM				
3:30 PM				
4:00 PM				
4:30 PM				
5:00 PM				
5:30 PM				
6:00 PM				
6:30 PM				
7:00 PM				

Playbook Exercise 19 - Activity Planner (see p. 47)

Strategic Project #1—This should be a specific, measurable task that can be achieved by leveraging the critical success from prior part of the Off-Season Playbook.

Expected Results—Identify the outcomes of this strategic project. These outcomes, if achieved will determine the success of the project.

Target Date to Achievement—Identify the timeline for achieving these results.

Required Tasks—This is the step-by-step process that will be used to achieve the desired results.

- _____

- _____

- _____

- _____

- _____

- _____

- _____
- _____
- _____
- _____
- _____
- _____

Strategic Project # 2 —This should be a specific, measurable task that can be achieved by leveraging the critical success from prior part of the Off-Season Playbook.

Expected Results—Identify the outcomes of this strategic project. These outcomes, if achieved will determine the success of the project.

Target Date to Achievement—Identify the timeline for achieving these results.

Required Tasks—This is the step-by-step process that will be used to achieve the desired results.

- _____

- _____
- _____
- _____
- _____
- _____
- _____
- _____
- _____
- _____
- _____

Strategic Project # 3 —This should be a specific, measurable task that can be achieved by leveraging the critical success from prior part of the Off-Season Playbook.

Expected Results—Identify the outcomes of this strategic project. These outcomes, if achieved will determine the success of the project.

Target Date to Achievement—Identify the timeline for achieving these results.

Required Tasks—This is the step-by-step process that will be used to achieve the desired results.

- _____

- _____

- _____

- _____

- _____

- _____

- _____

- _____

- _____

- _____

- _____

- _____

Strategic Project # 4 —This should be a specific, measurable task that can be achieved by leveraging the critical success from prior part of the Off-Season Playbook.

Expected Results—Identify the outcomes of this strategic project. These outcomes, if achieved will determine the success of the project.

Target Date to Achievement—Identify the timeline for achieving these results.

Required Tasks—This is the step-by-step process that will be used to achieve the desired results.

- _____

- _____

- _____

- _____

- _____

- _____

- _____

- _____

- _____

- _____

- _____

- _____

Strategic Project # 5 —This should be a specific, measurable task that can be achieved by leveraging the critical success from prior part of the Off-Season Playbook.

Expected Results—Identify the outcomes of this strategic project. These outcomes, if achieved will determine the success of the project.

Target Date to Achievement—Identify the timeline for achieving these results.

Required Tasks—This is the step-by-step process that will be used to achieve the desired results.

- _____

- _____

- _____

The Off-Season for Financial Advisors

- _____
- _____
- _____
- _____
- _____
- _____
- _____
- _____
- _____

Exercises From Chapter Six

_____

Playbook Exercise 20 - Coaching Maximizer (see p. 50)

The Coaching Call/Meeting Maximizer

Complete and submit this form 24 - 48 hours prior to your coaching session with your achievement coach to gain maximum benefit from the coaching time!

My Name: _____

Today's Date: _____

Rank the Following Life Areas 1—10
(1 being the worst and 10 being the best)

Physical Health and Vitality:

Nutrition   Worst 1 2 3 4 5 6 7 8 9 10 Best

Structure and Flexibility   Worst 1 2 3 4 5 6 7 8 9 10 Best

The Off-Season for Financial Advisors

Physical Strength   Worst 1 2 3 4 5 6 7 8 9 10 Best

Aerobic and Endurance   Worst 1 2 3 4 5 6 7 8 9 10 Best

Relationships:

Family   Worst 1 2 3 4 5 6 7 8 9 10 Best

Work   Worst 1 2 3 4 5 6 7 8 9 10 Best

Friends   Worst 1 2 3 4 5 6 7 8 9 10 Best

Spiritual, Purpose and Destiny:

Connection   Worst 1 2 3 4 5 6 7 8 9 10 Best

Certainty   Worst 1 2 3 4 5 6 7 8 9 10 Best

Growth   Worst 1 2 3 4 5 6 7 8 9 10 Best

Contribution   Worst 1 2 3 4 5 6 7 8 9 10 Best

Significance   Worst 1 2 3 4 5 6 7 8 9 10 Best

Variety   Worst 1 2 3 4 5 6 7 8 9 10 Best

Financial:

Short Term Cash Flow   Worst 1 2 3 4 5 6 7 8 9 10 Best

Mid Range Income   Worst 1 2 3 4 5 6 7 8 9 10 Best

Long Term Income   Worst 1 2 3 4 5 6 7 8 9 10 Best

1. What have I accomplished since our last session?

2. What are some of my wins?

3. Were there any commitments that I made, yet didn't complete? If so, what were they and why?

4. Do I have any BIG distractions or challenges right now? If so, what?

5. Do I have any significant opportunities available to me right now? If so, what?

6. This week, I made _____ entries into my Personal Journal.

7. As a result of working with my coach:

• What do I have that is different as a result of my last coaching session (RESULTS)?

- What am I doing that is different as a result of my last coaching session (ACTION)?

- Who am I being that is different as a result of my last coaching session (CHARACTER)?

8. Today, I am grateful for:

Important! Confirming my next coaching appointment

Date: _____ Time: _____ & Time Zone: _____

Comments:

_____
_____
_____
_____
_____
_____
_____
_____
_____
_____
_____

Playbook Exercise 21 -
Client Review Agenda Template (see p. 51)

Client Review Agenda

Client   Date

What do you appreciate most about the service we provide you?
(FI and COI primer)

_____

_____

_____

_____

_____

What services can we provide to you that would benefit you better? (FI and COI primer)

_____

_____

_____

_____

_____

What other professionals are you working with that you essentially have a lot of respect for and value? Always interested in helping them help you and knowing who's who to refer to other clients? (Alliance Opportunities)

_____

_____

_____

_____

_____

What "must do's" now and in the future... and "want to do's" now and in the future?

_____
_____
_____
_____
_____

Do you have any concerns that your spouse or family are not prepared to adequately manage your investments in the event that you are not able to do so?

_____
_____
_____
_____
_____

Are you contributing the maximum amount to any pre taxed retirement plan? Example 401k, Simple IRA, Tax Sheltered Annuity.

_____
_____
_____
_____
_____

Do you have a retirement plan at a former employer that is not being serviced the way you expect?

_____
_____
_____
_____
_____

What areas would you like to take action on before our next meeting?

___ Do I have enough life insurance
___ What if I get disabled
___ Assets protected from Nursing Home
___ Cancer Insurance
___ Roth IRA
___ IRA
___ Alternative to low interest rates
___ Funding my children's college
___ Will I have enough money to retire
___ Managing Debt
___ Retirement Plan for Business
___ Long-term investing
___ Social Security Benefits
___ Protect my Identity
___ Individual Health Insurance
___ Group Health Insurance
___ Succession Planning for Business

Looking out over the balance of both your lives, are you highly confident that your retirement income will always be enough to sustain your lifestyle, or are you at all concerned that at some point, in your retirement, you may start to run out of money?

How often would you prefer we connect?

Daily   Weekly   Monthly   Quarterly   Annually

What is the best way for us to connect?

Phone In-person Email Text Fax Letter Facebook Twitter

Would you like to be included in our weekly newsletter?

Yes   No

Wrap up with NEXT STEPS concerning gaps and opportunities.

Playbook Exercise 22 -
Favorable Introduction Script (see p. 52)

Ideal Client Favorable Introductions

Name of referring party

Telephone

"Mr./Mrs. _____ , you may not realize how difficult it is to make yourself known in our industry. Compliance and regulatory restrictions seriously hinder our ability to promote ourselves publicly these days. That's why I continue to count on my best clients introducing me to others who may want to know who I am, what I do and how I can help when the time is right. I'm simply looking for introductions to people like you, who are...

- Fun and easy to work with

- Open to advice and coachable

- Are successful

- Will appreciate help in reaching their goals and improving their situation

We both know most of the people you introduce me to are currently using some form of advisor so my desire is to simply introduce myself and my services so when the time is right, they know how I can help and how to connect. As you know, I do my best work with people like yourself with:

- Financial complexities

- Multiple homes/properties

- Kids in college

- Retirement interests – succession, exist strategies, etc.

154

- Business owner issues

- Potential tax burdens and a desire to maximize their long term wealth

So when you think of these attributes, what names come to mind? Let's list the names and telephone numbers of three qualified people who you would like to see us help with this type of profile.

          Name   Telephone

1.

2

3.

Thank you for your confidence in me and taking the time to help others reach their financial goals. Next steps…

How would you feel most comfortable introducing me to _____ (ask this for each referral)?

- In person – coffee, lunch, golf, etc.

- On phone – right now??

- Email – cc you

- Educational event/Seminar

- Card

How would you actually introduce me (ask this for each referral)?

- Who you are.

- Few ways they've benefited from your help.

- When this name came to mind, what was it that suggested this would be a good person to work with? As they answer, pick up the words they use as a 'script" for them to use with the prospect.

- Nature of the introduction – wanting to put a face with a name and provide another resource for valuable financial advice.

Accountability, Action, and Achievement

Exercises From Chapter Seven

Create Your MAP - Momentum Action Plan (see p. 56)

Company Name: _____

Fiscal Year: _____

Vision:

_____
_____
_____
_____
_____

Mission:

_____
_____
_____
_____
_____

The Off-Season for Financial Advisors

Values:

Value 1

_____

Value 2

_____

Value 3

_____

Value 4

_____

Value 5

_____

Focus Areas:

_____
_____
_____
_____
_____

KPI's:

_____
_____
_____
_____
_____

Strategies:

_____
_____
_____
_____
_____

Projects:

_____
_____
_____
_____
_____

Critical Activities:

_____
_____
_____
_____
_____

What did you learn about yourself as a result of this investment of your time?

What are you most grateful for today? Why?

If you were to win "The Big Game," what does that look like to you?

In 1 Year?

In 5 Years?

In 10 Years

Thank you for your participation! Do you have any final comments?

***The ProAdvisor Coach library of activities is also available in an easy-to-understand–and-use online format, enabling any Advisor to access their content areas between or during a coaching session. But don't worry, it's also secure. After all, we understand confidentiality is key! Our Off-Season program also enables us to guarantee excellent coaching delivery in the unlikely event that one of our coaches is unable to continue working with a client. The client's action steps are simply retained online in a secure location. To learn more: www.ProAdvisor Coach.com/offseason.